Education and Race

Education and Race

**An Analysis of the
Educational Production
Process**

Eric A. Hanushek

Lexington Books
D.C. Heath and Company
Lexington, Massachusetts
Toronto   London

To Nancy

Contents

List of Tables

Preface

Education is an emotional topic, evoking the hopes, dreams, tensions, and fears of American society. The promises of education—income and social status—interact with the costs of education—taxes and time—to produce intense concern about the management of the educational system. However, concern is not enough. There must be an understanding of what is desirable in school system operations. Without knowledge of how schools go about educating students it is not possible to make rational decisions about the structure of the system.

Many people have found condemnation of public schools to be both easy and salable; society seems ready, indeed eager, to read about the failure of schools. There is even an indignant tone of communication that is reserved for discussions of schools. But the next step, providing some guidance for redirection of school efforts and resources, proves to be a harder one to take. The next step is in fact the somewhat ambitious goal of this book. And, while the book may realistically fall quite short of definitive answers to the perplexing educational policy questions facing us, it does provide some insights into paths of investigation which appear profitable.

From the title it is obvious that a central concern of the study is the education of minorities in the United States. Minority incomes are systematically lower than the white incomes; their jobs are worse; their life expectancy is less; and so forth. Education is often seen as the cure. But is the educational system capable of doing the job? Chapter 1 delineates the past record of the educational system in equating the educational levels of whites and minorities. It also sets the background of the educational system in terms of the dynamics of urban areas and the financial problems faced by school systems.

Within chapter 2 the basic concepts of production relationships for education are described. Such input-output relationships provide a basic method for organizing what we know about the educational process. From a production function, it is possible to make decisions about educational policy. This chapter both describes the decision rules which administrators should use and presents a conceptual model of the educational process.

Chapters 3 through 5 illustrate how data from the past operations of the school system can be used to gain insights into the educational process. Statistical models representing the educational process in elementary schools are developed. These models provide a method of comparing the educational possibilities facing the school systems. In chapter 3 separate analyses are presented for the education of whites (by social class) and Mexican-Americans within one school system. Chapters 4 and 5 contain analyses of a sample of urban schools in the Great Lakes and Northeast regions for whites and blacks.

Chapter 6 looks into the question of school desegregation in some detail. The implications of racial and ethnic composition in earlier chapters are related to current discussions of the educational value of desegregation.

Finally, an attempt is made in chapter 7 to outline how such an analysis provides inputs to the educational decision maker. This discussion is provided more as an example of methodology than as a call for action. The complexities of education are so great and our knowledge of education so small that it would be foolhardy to take the conclusions as gospel. Instead this work represents some crude results and indicates where research in this area should be directed.

This study has received financial support from the Carnegie Corporation of New York in a grant to the Harvard Seminar on the Equality of Educational Opportunity Report (SEEOR), from the Economic Development Administration in a grant to the Harvard Program on Regional and Urban Economics (Project No. OER-015-G-66-1), and from the RAND Corporation and the Carnegie Corporation of New York (RPN 7502/7510).

Many people have contributed significantly to this study through comments and suggestions. And, while it is difficult to acknowledge all of the intellectual debts that have been built up, a few, especially large ones demand recognition. The general subject area was first introduced to me by Professor John Kain, and for that plus continued help, encouragement, and criticism I find that the largest acknowledgment possible here is indeed much too small. Many of the original ideas for this study were developed in the SEEOR discussions and I offer my thanks to both the organizers, Professors Daniel Patrick Moynihan and Thomas Pettigrew, and the many participants of that seminar. Various parts of the manuscript were markedly improved by suggestions from Professors Samuel Bowles, Franklin Fisher, John Jackson, Herbert Kiesling, Henry Levin, Edwin Kuh, Frank Sloan, and Finis Welch. Further, as is true in most educational endeavors, the intellectual quality of one's environment cannot be neglected; thus, general thanks go to Wayne Yeoman, Charles Wolf, and Nancy Hanushek for providing a suitable climate for such an undertaking. Finally, the three people who produced readable copies of manuscripts under severe time pressures—Gretchen Jackson, Joyce Watson, and Eleanor McStay—deserve special recognition.

Eric A. Hanushek

Washington, D.C.
May 1972

Education and Race

1 Topics in Public Education

The public schools of the United States have become the meeting ground—or perhaps battleground—of many social forces in society. Individuals of all political persuasions see schools as an important instrument of social development and call upon all parts of our political machinery—executive, legislative, and judicial—to bring about change in the schools. And, interestingly, change is almost always desired. Critics of the current schools are plentiful; defenders are noticeably few.

The outward appearance of the attacks on schools varies. In one arena there is the school financing battle which has surfaced in school bond issue referendums, court decisions, and various commission reports. In another arena, there are the struggles over control of schools, cloaked partly in the legal shroud of de jure and de facto segregation. These latter struggles are manifest in the courtroom, in school board elections, and in pressures to decentralize school administrations. Overlaying these specific, direct attacks on schools is an enormous amount of public debate, both in popular form and professional form, about general issues of school policy.

The confluence of these essentially negative views about our public school system has led to some basic attitude changes as concerns schools. Going into the decade of the sixties, in the aftermath of the Sputnik launching, considerable attention was given to the public schools. And, while Sputnik was taken as evidence that some school reforms were needed, there was a general feeling that the school system was up to the job. Embued with a national purpose, considerable support for increasing our commitment to the educational system was evident, and few people doubted that more schooling expenditures were the answer. But, by the end of the sixties, this general euphoria had dissipated to the extent that winning the moon race had virtually no impact on societal judgments of the sad state of the public school system. The present tone of thought about the educational system is captured by the report of the President's Commission on School Finance:

The system which has served our people so long and so well is, today, in serious trouble, and if we fail to recognize it, our country's chance to survive will all but disappear.[1]

Statements such as this, which are not difficult to find in current evaluations of schools, must be put into context, however. Certainly in terms of the specific subject matter taught in schools, there have been enormous improvements in education. Material previously reserved for college level instruction is now routinely covered in high schools. And, changes in instructional material now make many parents ill-equipped to help children with their school homework. Further, the frequent warnings and condemnations tend to imply that the problems of schools are very recent. Yet, it is difficult to perceive any dramatic changes in schools which make them suddenly on the verge of collapse (if they weren't a decade or two ago).

It is necessary to look elsewhere for the source of dissatisfaction and distrust of schools, and, along these lines, the most logical and persuasive explanation lies in societal changes. The reference system in which schools have been operating has clearly been changing, and schools, continuing to operate as they had in the past, now are judged differently. In particular, individuals and society perceive other uses of funds and are becoming more reluctant to devote increasing resources to schools—perhaps because they are not sure that school quality increases have kept pace with school expenditure increases. Secondly, while there has been an awareness that all individuals do not share equally in the rewards of society, it was always assumed that public schools acted to ameliorate some of the differences that would otherwise exist. This has been increasingly questioned.

These changes are closely related to the major conflicts in which schools are currently embroiled and suggest that efficiency of resource allocation and distribution of educational services are the heart of the critical issues in public education today. Each is the center of considerable concern, controversy, and emotion. Even though public elementary and secondary education consumes over $40 billion annually, there is very little knowledge about the educational process itself, and, thus, it is exceedingly difficult to insure the efficient use of funds available for education. And, since education is closely related to success in our society, the distribution of educational services plays a crucial role in deciding the distribution of jobs and income among individuals and groups.

The areas of resource allocation and distribution of educational services are very broad and complex. The goal of this study is to provide some insights into these areas, but, necessarily, only a fraction of the total set of problems can be analyzed. The focal point of this analysis is the specification and estimation of models of the educational production process. Such models provide insight into both educational issues since the relationship between inputs and educational output is central to any discussion of efficiency or equalization of educational benefits. Thus, this study offers a starting point in a complete analysis of the larger efficiency and distribution issues.

Resource Allocation

Resource allocation is not a trivial matter in the case of school systems. In a loose sense, people want "more" education. However, school systems must do their job in the face of increasing budgetary pressures. In metropolitan areas, both the central cities and the suburbs feel the budgetary squeeze, albeit for different reasons.

Central cities have experienced considerable changes in structure within the last two decades. There has been the flight to the suburbs of both population and industry.[2] However, the population movement has been quite selective with middle- and upper-income families moving out, to be replaced, in turn, with an in-migration of the rural poor. While central city total population has tended toward stability, the mixture of the population has changed. The changes in income distribution and employment patterns have lowered the fiscal ability of many central cities.[3] This has been accompanied by *increases* in the demands for many public services such as welfare, health, and fire and police protection. Thus, when revenues are becoming more difficult to raise in the central cities, competition for available revenues has increased.

The patterns in suburban communities has generally been different, but the effect has been the same: increased budgetary pressure on school systems. The rapid decentralization of population has been the heart of the suburban situation. Rapid growth requires sudden increases in many areas of public service: education, sanitation, fire and police protection. When financing is done through property taxes, large increases in tax rates often result.

Also, where debt limits on localities exist, governments often require a referendum vote to gain approval for expenditures.[4] The trend in school bond referendum votes is particularly interesting. As shown in table 1-1, there has been a dramatic drop in public support—at least relative to schools' hopes—over the past few years. By 1970, only half of the bond issues proposed could pass a referendum test.

Table 1-1
Approval on School Bond Elections, 1962-1970

| | Percentage Approved | |
Year	By Number	By Value
1962	72.2	68.9
1963	72.4	69.6
1964	72.5	71.1
1965	74.7	79.4
1966	72.5	74.5
1967	66.6	69.2
1968	67.6	62.5
1969	56.8	46.6
1970	53.2	49.5

Source: Richard H. Barr and Irene A. King," *Bond Sales for Public School Purposes 1969-70*," National Center of Educational Statistics (Washington: Government Printing Office, 1971).

Certainly part of the referendum defeats and, in fact, part of the budgetary pressures seen by schools are manufactured by the schools themselves. Schools with their ever-large appetites have been continually expanding their claim on national resources. Total expenditures on elementary and secondary education as a percentage of gross national product went from 2.0 percent in 1950 to 3.8 percent in 1968. Between 1960 and 1968, current expenditures per pupil increased at an annual rate of 7.3 percent—considerably above the rate of inflation for those years. However, part of this trend in nonsupport of school expenditures probably relates to dissatisfaction with school operations and the perceived rate of quality increase relative to expenditure increase.

Budgetary pressures tend to dramatize the need for efficient operation of public school systems. Certainly efficient allocation of resources—maximum educational output from a given set of resources—is always a goal. However, the need for efficiency becomes more obvious when school systems are faced with increased public pressure.

Efficient operation of schools is not simply a local problem. Since over half of the school bill is paid with state and national funds, there is considerable interest at higher levels of government in the efficiency of local school operations. While there are some theoretical analyses which demonstrate that properly constructed grants to local governments can lead to efficient expenditures, they tend to neglect most of the significant practical impediments to efficient operation.[5] In fact, local school efficiency may become more important to the federal and state governments as pressures mount to alter the existing system of school finance.[a]

Distribution of Educational Services

The second issue in public education today is the distribution of educational services. It is widely accepted that education is a necessary, if not a sufficient, condition for success in our society. Many studies have shown a high correlation between education and personal income, with a causal relationship from educational attainment to income frequently implied. If such is the case, discrimination in the provision of education is tantamount to unequal economic opportunity.

The key to the whole discussion of distribution is the concept of equity. Education differs from a pure public good in that individuals can be excluded from its consumption; a school board can prescribe the entire distribution of services. De jure segregation is an extreme case of this, but there are other forms of unequal distributions and exclusions of individuals. By determining the distribution of education, governments can then have a considerable impact on the distribution of income.

---

[a]One of the most frequently discussed reforms of the school finance system is full state funding of local schools.

There are several ways in which one might look at the distribution of educational services, or under the now-popular rubric, equality of educational opportunity. The two most obvious approaches are to ascertain whether all individuals receive the same school inputs or whether the equality should be in terms of outputs from the educational process. The input approach, largely motivated by legal discussions, assumes a much more limited goal since large differences in preparedness are known to exist among children entering school. These differences, which are also highly correlated with family background, imply that the simple equating of school inputs will yield very divergent outputs at the end of the educational process. Output equality, the second approach, takes a much broader view of the educational process and assumes that children should enter the job market at the end of school with the same opportunities. (Discussion of the output approach is necessarily less precise. Since ability differences among children at the individual level are large and since such innate differences are generally not the object of public policy, it is necessary to go to a concept of group equality of outputs, such as that between blacks and whites.)

The choice of definitions for equality of educational opportunity is subject to considerable controversy. However, output equality appears to be more consistent with our democratic values and, therefore, a proper long-range goal even though equality of inputs is a more immediately feasible and necessary policy.

While there are many possible dimensions in which the distribution of educational services can be analyzed, differences by race and ethnic background loom as by far the most important. Other stratifications of the population—regional, urban-rural, central city-suburb, or rich-poor—present some interesting problems, but the racial distinction is primary in terms of urgency for present public policy. Minorities suffer more in terms of education than any other possible groups of study. They are, in addition, subject to discrimination in other sectors of society.

Education is often cited as the way out of the circle of discrimination and poverty faced by the minority groups, even though the present school structure does not appear to be promoting such a solution to discrimination.

Differences in the distribution of education by race are not imaginary. In pure quantity terms for 1970, the median black over twenty-five years old had completed 9.9 years of school as compared to 12.2 years for the median white over twenty-five years old.[6] There are some changes in the specific numbers for different subsets of the population, and the differences are narrowing over time. (In 1970, the median years of school for blacks between the age of twenty-five and twenty-nine was 12.2 years, within half a year of comparable whites). The qualitative impressions remain the same, however: blacks continue to complete less schooling.

The educational differences are even larger when one considers quality of education. By matching scores on standardized achievement tests for different grade levels, it is possible to gain some indication of the magnitude of educational disadvantage in quality terms. Table 1-2, abstracted from the

Table 1-2

Achievement Differentials by Race and Region; Average Grade Levels Behind the Average White in the Metropolitan Northeast, Verbal Ability

	Grade Levels Behind		
Race and Region	Grade 6	Grade 9	Grade 12
White, nonmetropolitan			
South	.7	1.0	1.5
Southwest	.3	.4	.8
North	.2	.4	.9
White, metropolitan			
Northeast	—	—	—
Midwest	.1	.0	.4
South	.5	.5	.9
Southwest	.5	.6	.7
West	.3	.3	.5
Negro, nonmetropolitan			
South	2.5	3.9	5.2
Southwest	2.0	3.3	4.7
North	1.9	2.7	4.2
Negro, metropolitan			
Northeast	1.6	2.4	3.3
Midwest	1.7	2.2	3.3
South	2.0	3.0	4.2
Southwest	1.9	2.9	4.3
West	1.9	2.6	3.9
Mexican American	1.9	2.6	3.9

Source: *Equality of Educational Opportunity,* Table 3.121.1.

monumental report on U.S. education, *Equality of Educational Opportunity*, displays a comparative picture of education for blacks and whites in various regions as of 1965.[7] Using whites in the metropolitan Northeast as the standard, black twelfth graders in the urban Northeast are an average of 3.3 grade levels behind, which means that the blacks still in school at the twelfth grade are behind the average white in the ninth grade. The picture is even bleaker in other regions, reaching a pinnacle in the rural South where the average black in the twelfth grade is 5.2 years behind his white urban counterpart in the North. While there are some regional differences, it is obvious that being black is most important in quality terms. Thus, an adjusted median education figure which allowed for quality of education would present an even more alarming picture of racial differences than those previously presented. The picture is very similar for Mexican-Americans, who average four years (in quality terms) behind their white counterparts in the twelfth grade.

This must be taken in the context of society. There have been many studies that show considerable racial discrimination in the job market; the prevalence of ghettoes seems to provide ample proof of discrimination in the housing market. It is plausible that discrimination in the different sectors is more than a simple additive relationship and that educational deprivations magnify the problems. Such interdependencies, if they exist, would constitute prima facie evidence that the racial dimension is the most important dimension of the distribution of educational services.

Finally, in terms of political necessity, resolving minority educational problems seems to be crucial. Educational problems have been central in the civil rights movement and remain a major grievance of the black community. This is well documented in the *Report of the National Advisory Commission on Civil Disorders.*[8] The racial dimension is the most volatile political aspect of the distribution of educational services. Pressures for rectifying the imbalance in education are mounting and are becoming more urgent.

Thus, throughout this study, the subject of distribution of educational services is considered synonymous with the study of differences in educational services for whites and minority groups.

Production Functions for Education

While there are many possible ways to analyze the problems of resource allocation and the distribution of educational services, the analytic framework provided by the economist's concept of a production function appears to provide the most useful starting point. A production function describes the relationship tracing the maximum possible output level for a given set of inputs. This is a natural basis for making allocation decisions. It also provides a method of assessing the importance of differences in school inputs supplied to different groups (for example, blacks and whites) and ascertaining how educational inputs can efficiently be adjusted to rectify adverse distributions in educational output.

So-called production functions in education differ from those found in the economic theory of the firm. The production functions in economic literature are usually defined in terms of goods or tangible articles. Inputs to the educational process are, on the other hand, quite different from the traditional labor and capital that enter "normal" production functions. Part of the set of inputs are abstract quantities, such as attitudes, and these cannot be purchased in the market. Moreover, the output is itself a service. These differences do not, however, nullify the usefulness of the concepts of the production function in studying education.[b]

The principle feature of the production function relevant to the analysis of the efficiency and distribution questions is the mapping of the output possibilities for a set of inputs. For policy purposes certain groups of inputs (generally

---

[b]The concept and uses of production function are discussed in detail in chapter 2.

those which can be purchased in the market) are more interesting than others. The production function allows analysis of these sections while accounting for other inputs to the process (such as family background) which cannot be controlled readily by the policy maker.

Directions of Analysis

The focal point of this study is the specification and estimation of educational production functions where educational outputs are defined in terms of standardized test scores. The basic motivation for this evolves from the previously discussed questions of resource allocation and distribution of educational services. However, little effort is made at direct application of the production functions to specific aspects of these general problems. The models of the educational process which are analyzed are necessarily very simplified views of the actual complex process. It is difficult to use the estimated functions to make precise statements about the efficacy of individual projects. Nevertheless, the models give a useful portrayal of public education and the relationships between inputs and educational output.

Chapter 2 presents a conceptual model of the educational process. This model provides insights into what data are needed and what kinds of results may be expected; additionally, this chapter outlines how models of the educational process can be used in improving decision making in public schools.

Two separate empirical analyses of elementary schools are presented. Elementary schools are more desirable for this analysis since the structure of the school organization is generally simpler, the curricula more standardized, and the size more homogeneous than in secondary schools. There are obvious reasons to take advantage of simplifications in the institutional structure when attempting to model a process as complex as the educational production process. With ideal input data, which are not available, modeling the educational process within a comprehensive high school, or even a junior high, would be very difficult. There is simply little information about the process itself. Given the lack of information on the crucial issues of organization and curriculum, modeling the elementary school appears to be much more profitable than attempts at secondary schools.

The first analysis involves a relatively small sample of data for individual third graders in one school system. This sample was designed specifically to overcome the more important data problems which existed in other samples. However, by virtue of involving only one school system, it is difficult to generalize any of the results. The second sample, drawn from the data for *Equality of Educational Opportunity*, looks across many school systems in the Northeast and Great Lakes region. While this enlarged sample is useful in terms of generalizing about public school education, these data have many problems associated with them.

However, the consistency of results for the two analyses implies that the data limitations of both are not so great as to negate the usefulness of such studies.

A central concern throughout the analysis is the racial and ethnic context of public education. Particular attention is paid throughout the modeling efforts to the identification and analysis of racial aspects of the educational process. Since many of the most important issues in education revolve around these aspects, special care was taken to reduce any modeling errors in the dimension of racial composition of the schools and behavioral differences between whites and minorities. Specific attention is focused on the black population and the Mexican-American population.

2

A Conceptual Model of the Educational Process

From an unpretentious beginning in the early sixties, studies of the educational process have quickly achieved legitimacy in the realm of public policy analysis. Propelled by the *Coleman Report* and the ensuing controversy which surrounded that document, studies of input-output relationships in education now occupy a central position in public policy debates, in court cases, and in general thinking about educational issues.[1] But such studies are still in their infancy, and there remains considerable confusion—both in the minds of analysts and users—about the conceptual and methodological underpinnings of this line of inquiry. This chapter is aimed at clarifying the issues surrounding the analysis of the educational production process.

The immediate stimulus for preparing or using an input-output analysis of education may come from a variety of sources: budgetary pressures, parental dissatisfaction, racial tensions, or a court case. The overriding objective can be succinctly stated, however, as simply a desire to improve decision making within the educational sector. This chapter presents a general decision making framework, borrowed from the economic theory of production, which can be applied to managing the educational system. Within this framework a conceptual model of the educational process is presented to help organize our observations about schools and education in a way that is useful for policy purposes. This is not supplied as an exercise in abstract reasoning, but as a way of guiding the analysis of educational experiences. In this vein, the discussion is skewed toward empirical application since the gains in the analysis of education appear largest in that direction.

The decision making process that we are concerned with in this book focuses on the rational hiring, use and, in some cases, accommodation of inputs to the educational process. School decision makers—whether teachers, principals, superintendents, or what have you—actively affect the level of some educational factors, such as the quantity and quality of teachers, and passively accept other inputs, such as the student's home life. But while their job involves selecting a set of inputs into the educational process of students, they have a different set of objectives by which effectiveness as an administrator is judged.[a] These

---

[a]This may seem trivial, but there does seem to be a considerable amount of confusion on this matter, even among professional educators. Frequently, the quality of education is expressed in terms of expenditures per pupil or average class size. Yet these are inputs to the process, not outputs of the process. Certainly, there is an implicit hypothesis of a relationship between these inputs and educational output, but it remains an empirical question. Until it is demonstrated that such relationships exist, it is a strange measure of education. Moreover, it thoroughly obfuscates the real point of concern—educational output.

11

objectives include the achievement of a desired level of education for each student and the achievement of these levels at minimum costs, or the efficient operation of the school.[b]

Meeting these objectives in turn depends upon two factors: (1) knowledge of the relationship between inputs and outputs of the educational process; and (2) a decision rule to connect costs of various inputs to the process with their educational outputs.

At the outset, it is important to note that there is another concern which, while somewhat related, is not explicitly discussed within the development of decision rules for the efficient operation of schools. This aspect is the decision on the distribution of education among students. It is not omitted in the subsequent development because it is unimportant, but instead because it is not amenable to the same sort of economic analysis. For most of this analysis, the difficult equity decisions about the distribution of educational services among students are assumed to have already been made. It is noted only in passing here that knowledge of the educational process may be important in analyzing some distributional problems. This is the case when different relationships between inputs and outputs, or different production functions, hold for identifiable populations—say blacks and whites. Then, for a given distribution of inputs such as a fixed supply of teachers, the production functions aid in achieving efficient allocations of resources among groups. Since this is a fairly simple extension of the theoretical analysis and since it rests largely on an empirical question, the implications of this distributional question are not developed here.

A Simple Decision Rule

Education is usefully viewed as a production process. Through various psychological and physiological mechanisms a variety of inputs (smiling teachers, concerned parents, interesting friends, etc.) is combined to produce a given state of learning. The analogy to the production process in a firm, where a set of technical relationships determines the output which can be produced from a given combination of men and machinery, is immediately obvious.

The analogy between the educational process and a general production process is developed in order to profit from the extensive theoretical and empirical work that has already been done on the economics of production. Economic theory capitalizes on the conceptual construct of the "production function" to derive a set of decision rules for efficient use of inputs. Past empirical studies in economics further give some indication of profitable ways to proceed in the actual analysis.

---

[b]Efficient use or efficiency appears to have bad connotations in education. Economic efficiency implies achieving a given goal at minimum cost or, equivalently, maximizing the output for a given expenditure on inputs. This is considerably different from an unconstrained minimization of costs.

The formal decision rule presented in this section gives considerable insight into important aspects of the analysis. Even though our knowledge of the educational process is too meager to apply the rule with much precision, the delineation of the desired information provides guidance in the specification and interpretation of any estimated input-output relationships.

The economist's version of an input-output relationship, the production function, has long been part of economic theory.[2] In its simplest form, a production function is a technical relationship which can be used to calculate the level of output which can be attained from given quantities of inputs to a production process. Moreover, it is a special type of relationship, for it describes the *maximum* output which is technically feasible from a given set of inputs.

In both the general production process and the specific application to education, attention is focused on the amount of various inputs used in producing an output and not on the specific technical aspects underlying production. Thus, while the process of memory or assembly line layout affects the output level, they are not the central concern here. The individual in the educational process and the production plant in the general case are black boxes which are not explicitly opened in this analysis. As long as there exists stable learning relationships or a stable technology for the firm, there is no need to open the boxes to obtain answers to the questions of efficiency.

The maximizing aspect of the production function is quite important in formulating decision rules for the hiring of inputs. This feature allows calculation of an output level which is feasible from the best use of an additional amount of an input (or, alternatively, how much is lost when input usage is decreased). If the input-output relationship did not describe the maximum attainable output from a set of inputs, the effect on output of various changes in input configuration would be indeterminate.

The decision rule simply relates the cost of purchasing more of an input to the additional output received from adding the input and makes comparisons among the various inputs to the production process on the basis of input prices. While the price of additional input is often known, the amount of output that can be related to this added input is more difficult to ascertain.[3] Here is where the production function is needed. The production function yields the key decision-making element, the marginal product of each input. Marginal product is the amount of additional output received from using one more unit of a particular input when all other inputs are held at constant levels and all inputs are used in their most productive manner.[c] If the production function is known, marginal products can be determined mathematically through calculus or

---

[c]Marginal product *(MP)* is easily defined in mathematical terms. If the production process for the output, Q, calls for two inputs, K and L, and the production function is abstractly written as $Q = f(K,L)$, the marginal product is simply the first partial derivative of the output with respect to the given input. Thus,

$$MP_L = \frac{\partial Q}{\partial L} \text{ and } MP_K = \frac{\partial Q}{\partial K}$$

numerically by evaluating the output levels at two different levels of inputs.

Armed with the marginal product and price of each input, it is possible to devise a simple decision rule for hiring inputs. An efficient solution calls for equating the ratios of marginal product to price for all inputs into the production process.[d] This rule, which can be rigorously developed with calculus, has a certain amount of intuitive appeal. If the marginal product to price ratio for one input were higher than for all other inputs, it would pay to hire more of that input, since taking a dollar away from the hiring of other inputs and spending it on the "high productivity per dollar" input yields a net gain in output for the same cost.[e] It is very important to understand that the optimal hiring practice does not necessarily call for purchasing either the cheapest input or the most productive. The cheapest input might not add enough to output, and the most productive input may cost too much. In fact it is conceivable that the least productive or most expensive input is purchased if the ratio of marginal product to price is favorable.

This simple rule provides the means of rational (efficient) decision making. It also provides the motivation for the subsequent discussion of educational production functions. As will soon be apparent, however, the actual application of this rule to education is difficult because of our ignorance about the production function itself and its inherent complexity.

----

[d]To be technically complete, the rule given assumes diminishing marginal products. Diminishing marginal product is the commonly observed phenomenon that the additions to output from hiring additional units of an input *(MP)* decrease, although still remain positive, as more and more of the input is hired. It is also diminishing marginal products which allows one to equate the ratios, since the marginal product decreases as more is purchased, eventually bringing the "high productivity" input into line with the other inputs. This rule is derived from the maximization of output subject to a constraint on how much could be spent on inputs. From the previous footnote, if P_K and P_L are the prices of an additional unit of K and L, the rule is "hire inputs in such a manner that:

$$\frac{MP_K}{P_L} = \frac{MP_L}{P_L} \quad "$$

[e]A short, numerical example of this concept helps to clarify the situation. Assume Q, the output, is measured in terms of educs; K and L are measured in terms of units of capital and labor. From the production function we find that $MP_L = 10$ educs/unit of labor and $MP_K = 20$ educs/unit of capital. Finally, we know that the price of one unit of labor is \$1, and the price of one unit of capital is \$4. Given this situation, more labor should be hired since $MP_L/P_L = 10$ educs/dollar while $MP_K/P_K = 5$ educs/dollar. If one less unit of capital is used, the output decreases by 20 educs (the marginal product of capital) and \$4 is saved (the price of one unit of capital). If the \$4 is spent on labor, four additional units of labor input can be purchased and output increases by 40 educs. Thus, for the same expenditure, there is a net gain of 20 educs of output. In this example, an important point is made: the decision rule does not rest solely on the productivity of an input. Even though capital was more productive—that is, had a higher marginal product, more efficient operations could be had by decreasing the use of capital. (Note, however, that diminishing marginal products implies that this process of trading capital for labor will not always be advantageous. In fact, the net gain above may be less than 20 educs if MP_L decreases with the hiring of four more units of labor.)

Educational Production Functions

There would be little difficulty—and this book might not exist—if the school administrator could turn to an engineer for the precise specification of the production function for education. A mechanical application of the previous rule would then lead to efficient school operation. There is but one obstacle—educational engineers are difficult to find. In fact, considering the importance attached to education and the expense of running school systems, there has been surprisingly little theoretical or empirical investigation into the educational production process. Past research has provided some bits and pieces of the educational process, but never a completed picture.

One logical starting point in analyzing education would seem to be the field of learning theory.[4] But, while there exists a considerable body of literature under the topical description of learning theory, it provides little direct guidance in the production function and school policy context. The concentration upon relatively small-scope and complicated theories limits its usefulness for empirical application and makes it impossible to extract a framework for production function estimation from learning theory. Learning theory often attempts to open the black box of the production process. The questions which we are considering here generally do not go into the detailed classroom and interpersonal experience for which learning theory appears most applicable. Again, stability of the psychological aspects of learning and the detailed interactions is all that is required in order to analyze the more macro questions addressed here. (The preceding brief discussion is a little too cavalier with regard to learning theory. Much of our thought about education is tempered by aspects of learning theory. For example, notions of the cumulative nature of education, as discussed below, derive directly from discussions of reinforcement in the learning process.)

The separate works on developing production functions and on understanding of the educational process itself should actually be complementary, although the interchange between the two has been small because the research paths have been coincident with discipline boundaries. The production function analysis offers quick, aggregate clues about the operation of schools. It also pinpoints where research into the process is best placed. The process research, while often painfully slow, remains, however, one of the real hopes for long-run changes in the educational system. For example, effectively changing technologies, say to computer aided instruction, requires considerable insight into the educational process itself. Thus, even though this book abstracts from the details of the educational process, the synergetic nature of the two realms must be recognized.

Unfortunately, there is no single, comprehensive source providing an analytical framework for observing the educational production process. Guidance in educational research is forthcoming from a number of places, however. First, there has been considerable empirical research into various aspects of the educational problem. This fragmentary research provides a series of partial pictures which form a starting point and a series of initial hypotheses. Second, for what they are worth, there is an incalculable number of personal observations about education from lay and professional alike. Third, there is some guidance offered by related research such as economic analysis of production functions in various sectors. This latter is more important in the empirical study of education, but does provide some broad ideas useful in the conceptual formulation.

A Conceptual Model

The directions and scope of analysis are easiest to develop within the guidelines of a simple conceptual model of the educational process. (To call it a theoretical model at this state of knowledge would certainly be presumptuous.) Most students of education would accept a model of the educational process similar to Eq. 2.1.

$$A_{it} = g(F_i^{(t)}, P_i^{(t)}, I_i, S_i^{(t)}) \tag{2.1}$$

where A_{it} = vector, or multidimensional set, of educational achievement of the ith student at time t

$F_i^{(t)}$ = vector of individual and family characteristics for the ith student cumulative to time t

$P_i^{(t)}$ = vector of student body characteristics (peer influences), i.e., socioeconomic and background characteristics of other students in the school, cumulative to time t

I_i = vector of initial endowments of the ith student

$S_i^{(t)}$ = vector of school inputs relevant to the ith student cumulative to time t

In the abstract, it is difficult to quarrel with such a depiction. The equation simply states: The achievement of an individual (ith) student at time t [A_{it}] is some function [g] of his characteristics and those of his immediate family cumulative to time t [$F_i^{(t)}$]; of the characteristics of his peers [$P_i^{(t)}$]; of his initial endowments or innate abilities [I_i]; and of the quantity and quality of educational (school) inputs throughout his lifetime [$S_i^{(t)}$]. This model serves much the same purpose as the traditional economic theory specification of a production function that output is a function of capital and labor. It gives a starting point for analysis of production; controversy arises only after the model is further specified (that is, after the measures of capital and labor are specified.)

In the conceptual model, the four vectors, or groupings of inputs, could be defined differently; the way that the inputs to education are arrayed is not sacrosanct. The given groupings do seem preferable to alternatives, however, because the policy connotations within each vector are relatively homogeneous while the connotations between vectors are quite different. In fact, the arrangement of inputs into the four vectors brings into focus some of the sharpest controversies in education today, for example, compensatory education versus busing versus Headstart, longer school days, and longer school years. Thus, the breakdown of inputs represents more than an expositional device.

This abstract model introduces several useful concepts. For empirical analysis, the most important aspect of Eq. 2.1 is the emphasis upon the confluence of different inputs to education.[f] Education is not a product solely of the schools, nor solely of innate abilities, nor solely of nonschool environment. Instead, each of these elements contributes a part to the education of the individual. (In fact, Eq. 2.1 should actually be written in a more general form so that some output quantities can have an effect on other outputs. For example, reading ability may affect other educational outputs. Such a more general form will actually be considered in the application of the conceptual model.) The analytical design should focus on specifying each of these input groupings, not just one or two of them. The exclusion of any of the vectors from an analysis of the educational process must be carefully considered in terms of potential biases which would be introduced.

The role of time in the educational process is the second concept introduced in Eq. 2.1. The achievement of an individual at any particular point in time is dependent not only on educational inputs during that time period, but also on educational inputs of the past.[g] This cumulative nature of the educational process and, thus, the length of the period of production lead to some difficulty in the analysis of education. The relevant period of production appears shorter for other products than for education. For example, a home is constructed in ninety days while a Ph.D. takes twenty-five or thirty years. At the very least this long time period has many ramifications for input measurement and data collection during analysis. The complexity of time in educational production processes is partly due to structural (technological) differences with other production processes and partly due to the ambitions, interests, and data of those doing research in education. These latter factors indicate that a portion of this time difference is more illusory than real. Analysis of housing production begins with a certain level of refined materials that input to the process such as framing materials, cement, nails, trained labor, etc. If the growing of trees for

---

[f]Note that Eq. 2.1 says nothing about the types of interactions which exist among the vectors. Likewise, it says nothing about correlations which might exist such as the commonly observed phenomenon of better schools existing in better (upper class) neighborhoods. These interactions come with further specification.

[g]Time actually enters in two ways. Not only must we consider different inputs (say different teachers) that have historically entered the educational process, but also we must acknowledge that the inputs occurred over a time period and in a given sequence. Thus, having six teachers over a six year period is not equivalent to having the same six teachers in a one year period.

the framing materials was considered, the difference in length of production periods changes sign. Thus, the convention of looking at the entire period of formal schooling as the production period leads to some of this difference in apparent production times between education and other goods.

An initial level of educational achievement, A_{it*} can be introduced as a "raw material" into the educational process and when this is done, it is necessary to look only at inputs between time $t*$ and time t. Thus, Eq. 2.1 can be rewritten as Eq. 2.2.[h] Since the time period $(t-t*)$ can be made as small as one wants to make it, this specification can be used to reduce the period and, thus, the analytical complexities.

$$A_{it} = g*(F_i^{(t-t*)}, P_i^{(t-t*)}, I_i, S_i^{(t-t*)}, A_{it*}) \ , \qquad (2.2)$$

where the vectors are cumulative over the increment in time since $t*$.

This gambit, while simplifying the analytical tasks, does have drawbacks since the length of production period determines the range of policy issues which can be considered. Policies which are operative outside of the production period chosen $(t-t*)$ cannot be considered in the analysis unless the impact through A_{it*} is known. Therefore, the fact that educational analyses have tended to look at large time periods in part reflects ambition arising from an interest in many policy alternatives covering a wide time horizon.[5] (For example, an analysis of Headstart effects on high school achievement involves more than the range of formal schooling.)

Long periods of production present few conceptual problems. There is no difficulty substituting t equal to twenty-five years in Eq. 2.1 or 2.2. But, as intimated previously, the real concern with long production periods arises in attempts to specify the relationships more explicitly and to analyze them empirically. For a number of reasons, short time periods are preferred. Long time periods imply many more elements or variables in the input vectors than do short time periods. For most analyses, simplicity of the model is a virtue. Not only are simple models easier to interpret, but also the most commonly used empirical methods (particularly forms of regression analysis) are best suited to them.

A related issue is that the data collection and data organization problems grow at close to geometric rates over time. By the time a student is in the twelfth grade, he usually has had between three and four dozen separate teachers, has been to several schools, and has changed his future plans radically.

---

[h]Eq. 2.1 can be considered as a special case of Eq. 2.2 where $t* = 0$. It is possible to argue that the input vectors in Eq. 2.2 should still start at time 0 even though A_{it*} is included in the case of $t* > 0$. This argument would arise out of interactions between current learning ability and past influences (before $t*$), i.e., the precise combination of inputs that led to A_{it*} is important. However, the data requirements in this situation are increased considerably.

Collecting information on all of these and weighting the impact of each in producing A_{it} is an overwhelmingly large job. Even the largest computers are not capable of handling the extremely large data matrixes implied by very many individual observations of large input vectors. Therefore, the emphasis on the time aspect arises chiefly from practicality grounds rather than conceptual grounds. The most common research strategy is to proceed from easier to harder tasks, for the "easy ones" often turn out to be difficult enough.

Eq. 2.2 provides a rudimentary framework from which an educational production function can be developed. The usefulness of such a production function depends, of course, on how the vectors in the conceptual model are specified and measured. In particular, it is important to consider how different specifications reduce the ability to apply the decision rule given previously.

The ensuing discussion is not meant to be comprehensive in dealing with the details of applying the conceptual model to specific learning situations. Many of the actual empirical decisions involving the precise specification of a model of the educational process are pragmatic ones based upon the cost and availability of different kinds of data. Analytical decisions of this nature—for example, specific variable definitions—are reserved for the applications chapters which follow. The purpose of this chapter is to discuss general issues; that is, issues of motivation or possible analyses which have broader application and appeal.

The context for this discussion is important to understand. There are a variety of ways in which information about educational production functions could conceivably be gathered: I could tell you what I think it looks like; educators could be polled and their answers aggregated; or the U.S. Office of Education could proclaim an "official" production function. As an alternative, and the one accepted here, the past operations of schools can be observed and generalizations about their effects can be made through statistical analysis. In particular, student achievement and educational inputs will be measured—quantified if you like—and related to each other through regression analysis. Regression analysis, when properly applied, provides information about the effects on achievement of varying the amounts of different inputs, that is, the marginal products of different inputs. But regression analysis is not a panacea because the caveat "when properly applied" is often a binding constraint. A particularly vexing problem with regression analysis is the necessity of completely specifying the correct relationship between inputs and outputs before any statistical estimation is accomplished, or at least before it is properly accomplished. All of the variables must be measured and observed in order to arrive at good estimates of the marginal products of different inputs. This of course is a considerable burden given the current state of knowledge about educational production functions. This chapter distills some past knowledge about the educational production process to aid in specifying and interpreting estimated regression equations. Further, it attempts to indicate what happens if we go wrong in specifying particular parts of the model.

The Output of Education

The common statement that schools have many tasks to perform is another way of saying that schools are expected to produce a multidimensional output. While the job of the school is "to teach," this can have many meanings even among teachers. There has been a fair amount of literature concerning the expected outputs of the school, but it has not always been amenable to measurement for analytical purposes.[6]

The aim here is not to provide any new or particularly insightful views of the "goals of education." Those have been discussed, indeed overdiscussed, elsewhere. This section builds upon the simple observation that education can be appropriately viewed as an instrument of society—an instrument that transforms Stone Age infants into people capable of coexisting with and extending modern society.

The success of schools with any individual, then, undoubtedly relates to the individual's post-school position and behavior in society, and approaching an analysis of education from this starting point appears fruitful. Much of the attention paid to schools arises from the hypothesized relationship between education and future productivity of income. This is such a commonly accepted view that it hardly needs support. (Certainly the lure of future income is an important determinant of the schooling aspirations held by parents and students. And alumni income is an accepted rating of college and university quality.) Thus, one major category of school outputs, the "skill dimension," relates to the future economic impact of schooling. The second major category of school output is the development of societal values and norms. This includes developing behavioral standards, good citizenship, etc. These two broad categories, which are not entirely mutually exclusive, will be used as a basis for the subsequent discussion.

After minimal consideration, it is obvious that there is no consensus on a theoretically approved measure of the product of schools. Few discussions of schools are precise enough to provide operationally useful output definitions. Thus, throughout this discussion actual (obtainable) measures of output will be introduced both for clarity and to set the stage for subsequent empirical considerations.

Skill Aspects of Education

Education is viewed as a prime determinant of the productive capacity of an individual and, as such, an important factor in setting the economic level of each person. The skills a student acquires, including general cognitive development, basic reading and arithmetic, and specific subject matter, strongly influence his occupation and, therefore, his socioeconomic level.[7] Thus, the skill direction involves several different components, relating to different types of skills. These would include verbal ability, math ability and specific subject manner knowledge (including explicit vocational training).[8]

There are many simple measures of the skill aspects of schooling. School grades in basic courses and standardized ability and achievement test scores are aimed at measuring the depth of cognitive and subject area development. Alternatively, retention rates of school (the opposite of dropout rates) and college continuation measure length of schooling. Finally, future incomes or occupational status of the individual are direct measures of an individual's skills. While the list can be expanded to reflect more specific measures, this presents a representative grouping. Choice among alternative measures is often based upon pragmatic considerations of data availability, but there are some guidelines to aid in any choice.

First, in order to make generalizations about the educational process, objectivity is important. An essential ingredient of objectivity is a readily definable scale of measurement. Does the measure consistently tell what it purports to tell? With respect to the above list of possible standards, measures like basic course grades or grade failures which involve interteacher and interschool comparisons require careful interpretation, since they tend to use different scales. This makes generalizations from such quantifications of education quite difficult and prompts more attention to standardized measures such as achievement test scores or quantity of schooling.[9]

Second, the variety of measures emphasizes the fact that choice is related to viewpoint. It is possible to take the position that ignorance per se is bad and, thus, that education is a final product which represents a lessening of ignorance. In this case, almost any objective measure of attainment can be used without worry. But, this is not the prevalent view in the analysis of education. It if were, the intensity of feelings about education would be lessened considerably. Interest arises more from the view of education as an intermediate output, that is, an output which is used as an input in some other process such as production of goods in the economy. In this latter case the desired measure is the effect of the educational process on productivity (or income in a competitive economy). As a variant of this, the socioeconomic status of the individual can be considered as the final product, and the input of schooling can be evaluated relative to that. These latter viewpoints call for additional care in analysis and interpretation because not all conceivable measures of achievement reflect employable skill differences.

For operational purposes, when the issue is the hiring of inputs to the educational process, a measure which is a function of the desired final product will generally suffice, albeit with possible difficult interpretative problems. Thus, if there is a single valued relationship between say verbal ability test scores or years of schooling and income, the choice of output measures is largely one of convenience and data availability. (For other purposes, such as analyzing the level of investment in education as opposed to just the hiring of inputs for a given level, more information about the transformation between test scores and income may be needed in order to meaningfully interpret the marginal products of the various inputs.[i] This, however, is not the immediate purpose in this analysis.)

One of the basic distinctions among potential output measures for education is whether the measure relates to quantity or quality of schooling. In most production processes analyzed by economists this consideration is never explicitly made since output quality is assumed to be constant. Economic theory is usually concerned with homogeneous physical goods. Education, though, more closely resembles a service and must be treated differently than a physical good. The first studies of education by economists were concerned solely with quantity of output as measured in years of schooling completed.[10] However, it has become more and more apparent that large quality differences do exist. For example, on standardized verbal ability tests, there is an estimated difference of five quality equivalent years of schooling between average northern whites and southern blacks in the twelfth grade, that is, groups with the same actual quantity of education.[11] In fact for the most part the previous discussion of outputs in this section has emphasized quality differences. Two specific output measures mentioned, though, were school retention rate and college continuation rate, which are pure quantity measures. In analyzing the educational process, how does the variance in both quantity and quality of outputs enter?

One conclusion that arises is that quantity and quality must generally be considered separately in analyses of the educational production process. Conceptually, it would seem possible to devise a test which combined quantity and quality. In point of fact, this has not been possible. Moreover, it may not be completely desirable. For some analyses, such as the relationship of education to income, it may be useful to develop quality equivalent years of school by adjusting school quantity for achievement test differences.[12] However, this is not a necessarily good measure of output when doing empirical research into the production function for education. The major shortcoming of such an approach is that it tends to confuse two, logically separable processes: (1) retention, and (2) education or the imparting of certain knowledge. Both aspects of education are important. Yet, they are very difficult to analyze together. Each places a different, and not completely compatible, set of requirements on the data collected and the analysis undertaken. This discussion, as with most recent work in the area, is concerned exclusively with quality aspects of education. The production of different quantities of education is in some sense a larger problem,

---

[i] It must be noted that education is not the only determinant of income. Other factors such as race, age, occupation, and region must be introduced in determining a relationship between education and income. For investment decisions the marginal income gains from additional schooling are important. There have been several studies which consider a total earnings relationship, some of which are mentioned in note 7.

for it involves many more nonschool aspects including attitude formation and the reward structure within society for additional quantities of education.[13] Being larger implies that the educational decision maker has less control over it. Further, there is some evidence that, if quality is accounted for, quantity may be relatively less important in determining income.[14]

One of the simplest, most convenient ways to handle quality is the reverse of the usual production analysis. Instead of looking at output of the same quality it is possible to look at output of the same quantity, that is, students who have completed the same number of years of schooling. Analysis then centers on the production of different qualities of output. In looking at education-income relationships, this implies looking at income distribution within the group that has completed the same number of years of schooling. With achievement scores, quantity is automatically held constant by looking at the same grade.

Finally, since standardized achievement scores have been emphasized as a possible measure of skill aspects of schooling and will be used exclusively in this study, it is propitious to bring up an old argument which is circumvented by placing ultimate attention on outputs such as income or social status to which achievement is an intermediate good. Ability and achievement tests have long been considered "culturally unfair," that is, they are biased toward reflecting things within the ken of middle-class Caucasian children, but not disadvantaged youth. But, to the extent that the middle-class skills measured by the test are the criteria which can be expected to be used in future hirings, promotions, etc., the cultural biases are an advantage, not a detriment. The relationship between job and middle-class attributes is demonstrated empirically by the correlations which have been found between test scores and income.[15]

Socialization Aspects of Education

At the other end of the output range lies the development of attitudes and values, or the socialization process. While socialization has many facets, the central element is the development of a set of behavioral norms which may include categories such as discipline, racial attitudes, morality, self-awareness, general attitudes, righteousness, responsible citizenship, etc.

The general behavioral concerns grouped under the category of socialization have traditionally fallen into the realm of psychological research. And in that context the analysis has not focused upon educational policy questions. Further, the importance of schools in the socialization process and the relationship between the behavioral characteristics produced through socialization and society remain largely unanalyzed and unknown. This section attempts to pull together the various issues which arise in terms of socialization vis-à-vis schools and society.[16]

The discussion of socialization within schools splits into two distinct streams.

These streams are easiest to differentiate in terms of their summary impression of socialization within schools, that is, whether socialization is basically producing "goods" or basically producing "bads."

The production of "goods" is directly related to the previous production function notions and will be considered first. The central thesis is that schools produce a range of attitude and value outputs that are related, as in Eq. 2.1, to a set of school and nonschool inputs, and that these outputs are valued by society. The exact measurement of these outputs has received considerably less attention than the skill portion, and, thus, the discussion is more tentative and suggestive. But a list of simple measures would include: school suspensions and expulsions, drug addiction rates, juvenile delinquency rates, citizenship test scores, voter participation rates, and various student attitude indexes, such as views about future education, race relations, or his ultimate role in society. This list could be expanded easily, but is presented more as an illustration of the range of possibilities than as an explicit guide to analysis.

Again in the socialization realm, education is viewed not as an end in itself, but as a contributor to the future role of an individual in society. Nevertheless, attempts to link the possible socialization measures with performance of individuals within society have not proceeded very far, and the choice among measures of socialization remains chiefly a conceptual one.

The other side of the socialization facet of schools—the "bad" side—has received considerable recent attention. There have been several concerned outcries about schools that relate to socialization, and these tend to be indignant, and often shrill, about the role of schools in attitude formations.

It should surprise no one that schools play an active role in socializing individuals and, in fact, while slightly surprised, the social commentators who discuss socialization in schools do not concentrate too much upon whether or not schools affect or even should affect students' values; instead, they concentrate upon the type of socialization and the distribution of values produced in schools. There is a mixture of hypotheses (but few precise measures) contained in what may be labeled the "reform" literature. This view suggests that schools produce docile, dull, obedient, diligent, uncreative students and that these characteristics are systematically distributed to preserve past social class patterns. (Different authors, of course, present different combinations of these hypotheses.)

This view of socialization is very much the antithesis of educational production function analysis (although it doesn't have to be). A strong statement of this overall view is that schools only perform a sorting role in which students are conditioned for certain positions in society, and that the skill development, or cognitive domain, is largely irrelevant. The exact motivations suggested for producing essentially undesirable behavioral characteristics and the distribution of these varies: bureaucratic rigidity, ineptness, social class conspiracy, etc., but those issues are not important at this point. This position requires attention because, if substantially correct, it considerably lessens the usefulness of the approach suggested throughout this book. But it is premature to think of choosing among the different views of schools. At the present time the evidence supporting the strong socialization position is scanty—indeed scantier than that supporting the general usefulness of production function analyses. Each view needs considerably more thought and analysis before it can be reliably compared with others. Further, it may be inappropriate to "choose." The strong ("bad") socialization hypothesis implies that the different outputs are dichotomous and tends to look on schools as producing either cognitive factors that are rewarded *or* behavioral patterns that are rewarded. A more general and currently more accepted position is that schools simultaneously produce skills, "good" social factors, and "bad" social factors. And this implies just what Eq. 2.1 implies—the production process must be viewed as multidimensional.

This cursory discussion of socialization is not meant to provide any real conclusions or judgments, only to relate a range of factors which need future attention. However, in contrast to the skill dimension, this socialization discussion can be carried no further here. The lack of data—a quite general problem in this area—precludes any attention to socialization aspects in the subsequent empirical chapters.

Joint Production

Multidimensional output from the educational process affects the decision rule developed to handle the hiring of educational inputs. The decision rule was developed from the simple case where there was one output from the production function. But, as discussed above, education is really a case of joint production—more than one output is produced by the same inputs. Clearly the previous decision rule must be modified because the decision problem with joint production involves deciding the appropriate inputs *plus* the appropriate mix of outputs. Up until now, it has been possible to avoid discussion of the total output level; with joint production this is impossible.

Economic theory does provide a new rule for efficient production in this joint production, but it is not useful to develop the modified rule formally at this time. The required modifications are easy to grasp intuitively—outputs are produced proportional to their relative value (or price in the general economic case). Further, input hiring decisions weight the production of more valuable outputs more heavily. This is only logical; radical adjustments in the hiring of inputs shouldn't be undertaken to produce better minor outputs such as, say, music appreciation.[17]

The best analytical strategy appears to be compromise between what is desirable theoretically and what is obtainable empirically. Complete and precise

application of the expanded decision rule requires considerably more information than is generally available. Prices, giving the relative value of different
outputs, are not "naturally" derived through markets for each dimension. And,
the possibility of analyzing several different dimensions of output is often
prohibited because of the nonavailability of the necessary data. At this stage in
knowledge a reasonable research strategy involves analysis of separate production functions for a variety of outputs with a pragmatic solution to the joint
production problem obtained by positing the relative importance of each output
measure. The exact solution depends upon the specific circumstances. For
example, if one dimension of output is agreed to be much more important than
all other dimensions (for example reading ability in elementary schools), then
the analyst would not go far wrong by concentrating attention on that
dimension. Alternatively, if there don't seem to be serious conflicts among the
inputs when looking at different outputs (in particular, important inputs are not
related positively with one output and negatively with another), looking at a
single output again may not be too damaging. Nevertheless, the appropriateness
of such assumptions cannot be considered in a wholly abstract manner, since
they rest on empirical questions—questions which are now only slightly understood. On the other side of the ledger, however, there is some comprehension of
the costs associated with not proceeding. These costs are derived from uncertainties in the efficient operation of a $40 billion per year system.

One point should be clarified here. Joint production has been mentioned by
others in a different context, namely its effect on statistical analysis. The
theoretical aspects and the empirical aspects of joint production are different,
however. There are some products of education which might not be valued
individually, but which input into the production of other outputs. An example
would be classroom discipline which mainly makes it possible for the teacher to
teach the desired output, say reading. To some extent, attitude formation fits
into the same category. These have implication for the empirical analysis, but
fall outside of the theoretical complications of joint production. The empirical
complication, to get ahead of the discussion, involves the effect of such a joint
output on statistical regression equation model. This calls for the use of special
techniques other than commonly used least squares regression analysis.

Inputs to Education

Discussing the inputs to the educational process on a conceptual basis is even
more difficult than the discussion of outputs. With very little theoretical analysis
to rely upon, most of the discussion is drawn from past empirical work into
various aspects of the educational process. This discussion is not meant to be
comprehensive, since much of the supporting work and the pragmatic analytical
decisions will be presented in the framework of actual application. The

discussion here serves to highlight issues in the application of the production decision rules to the types of statistical study which will be undertaken later in this book.

Family Background $[F_i^{(t)}]$

The role of the student's environment in education is unquestionably important. Even during the school year, the student spends more than half of his waking hours outside of the school. And it is tautological that during the very important preschool years the student spends all of his time outside of school. Nevertheless, while there is no disagreement about the importance—conceptually or empirically—of family background, accord over the character, measurement, and interpretation of family background factors cannot be assumed.

Several models of family influence apply to education. The family provides an example of verbal structure; a set of attitudes toward school, the community, and society; help in school work; a value system; goals; respect for authority; notions of discipline; and the purely physical environment including food and clothing. Some of these are direct inputs into the educational process while some are indirect in the sense that they provide the framework in which the educational process can be pursued.

While the underlying notions are fairly straightforward, devising good measures of them is a formidable task. Following individual students for some period of time and observing interaction with family and friends is generally infeasible—even if what was to be observed could be specified. Without direct measures of family inputs, interest centers on proxies or surrogates of the inputs listed.[j]

Among the list of proxies (based considerably on past empirical research) would be income level, the socioeconomic status (SES) of the family, parents' education, the number of people in the family, the family structure, languages spoken in the home, size of home, indices of parental interest in education, and so forth. The proxies tend to be as commonly known as the central hypotheses. At times they are even confused with the true concepts.

While it is not worthwhile to discuss the specific measures in detail, it is valuable to consider the family inputs vis-à-vis the decision rule for hiring inputs. The decision rule tells how much of an input should be purchased, given the price in the market and its effect on output, or its marginal product. But, the marginal products in the decision rule refer to the "true" variables—those which yield output changes when changed—and not to the proxy variables. And the

---

[j]As with the measurement of outputs, a proxy is a measurable variable which is highly correlated with the (unmeasurable) variable of interest. For describing past behavior, it is not necessary that the relationship will persist over time. In fact, as discussed below, it is quite conceivable that public policy could change the relationship between the proxy and the true variable.

array of qualities and interactions considered in the "true" family vector is not normally purchased in the market.

Amplifying further, while the proxies might involve market quantities (such as income level), the true concepts (attitudes, home education, etc.) either aren't easily purchased or their price is very high. Purchasing just the proxy attributes doesn't accomplish anything, because education is affected only if causal relationships exist. Take, for example, SES measures of family background. It seems reasonable that the causal relationship between the proxy measures of family inputs and achievement is quite low. To be sure, a production function using a proxy such as income level will yield "marginal products" by brute mathematics. However, this is not very helpful to the decision maker. Achievement may be raised through sudden changes in income if the income increase brings about a change in attitudes, better explicit education in the home, richer interactions, etc., but these changes in "real" inputs would not reasonably be expected to be large, at least in the short run. At a minimum one can conclude that it would be extremely expensive to attempt affecting educational achievement through large operations on family background. But, this is bordering on prejudgment of the actual form of the educational production function and the result of applying the decision rule and thus is properly left for later discussion.

One set of potential policies aimed at the family input to education does affect the focus of attention in an empirical analysis. These are programs, generally suggested as remedial programs to make up for educationally bad family inputs, which are explicitly designed to lessen the amount of family input. These include Headstart (getting them earlier), and lengthening the school day and school year (having them longer). Analyzing these requires care to be exercised in modeling the process since quantities of family inputs must be explicitly considered.

As a concluding remark, when looking at education from a policy point of view, the question of "relative importance" of family inputs (compared with other input vectors) is an inherently uninteresting question.[18] In particular, trying to divide (generally by analysis of variance) a given level of achievement between education in the home and education in the school does not provide useful knowledge to the decision maker. The interest is in the output of education. Thus, the legitimate question is how much additional input of one type is required to produce a specified change in output and what are the associated costs. The "relative importance" quest often has the goal of absolving the system from guilt—for if achievement differences come more from home than school, how can schools be held responsible? But importance as commonly viewed has little to do with the appropriateness of different public policies.

Peer Group Inputs $[P_i^{(t)}]$

There is more to a student's educational environment than just his family; there are his associates or peers. Peers enter into the educational process in a number of ways, influencing the individual student with respect to attitudes toward school, ambition, discipline, etc.; providing models of language usage and sources of specific subject information; and affecting directly the amount of teacher input in specific subjects. This last element reflects the externalities in the classroom due to both discipline effects and different rates of learning of individuals which affect the speed of the class in covering subject matter and the fact that teacher inputs will not be uniform among students within the same classroom. These issues are central to arguments for tracking or ability grouping of students within schools.

Since peer influences resemble collective impacts of influences like those existing in the family, many of the comments on empirical measures for the family vector hold. A peer vector would include appropriately aggregated vectors of the attitudes, backgrounds, and performances of other students and children which the individual comes into contact with. Empirically, this implies using aggregates of the proxy measures of home environment. Precision in formulating this vector would require considerable detailed information on friends and associates, more than could reasonably be expected. However, for most purposes simple averages of characteristics for classmates would not appear to be far from the desired.

For policy purposes the effects of peers are quite important. There exists considerable controversy today about the compositional effects of schools, particularly with regard to racial composition. This is pertinent to movements toward busing children out of neighborhoods, racial imbalance laws, and the general concern over de jure and de facto segregation of schools.[19] Certainly other issues—moral, ideological, political—are intertwined in the consideration of school composition, but the effect of different school and classroom compositions on achievement must be an important aspect of the discussion.

Peers fall into two groups—the inside school group and the outside school group. To the extent that school attendance is determined by geographic neighborhoods, this distinction is diminished in importance. However, when the student associates with different peers inside and outside of school, public policy analyses must often consider both groups, since peer influences are not completely synonymous with student body characteristics. This would, of course, be the case when school attendance is not determined by neighborhoods.

Initial Endowments [I_i]

Nearly everybody will agree that different individuals have different capacities or different abilities to learn, but the manner in which innate abilities might enter the educational production function is a subject of considerable controversy. The abstract specification is amenable to a variety of different genetic-environmental interactions, provided that measures of initial endowments exist. The distinction between conceptual desirability of an innate component and measurability must be made early. The inclusion of I_i in Eq. 2.1 is strictly on the conceptual grounds that genetic differences do exist among individuals and do appear to affect education, regardless of our ability to measure them. It is widely accepted that common measures such as an intelligence quotient (IQ) do not measure accurately the abstract endowments vector. Instead of a pure genetic input, these measures pick up both a genetic component and an environment of the child and do change over time.[20] Thus, even though such a concept may be desirable, we are unable to measure it directly.

If, as is currently the case in empirical work, no measure of initial endowments is available, is the possibility of empirical work on educational production functions foreclosed? The argument that it isn't follows two lines of thought. First, if there is mobility within our society (or at least within races) based upon ability and if initial endowments are in part hereditary, then initial endowments will be partially reflected by the socioeconomic status of the family. Without a measure of initial endowments the influence of family background will be exaggerated, but the model will approach the completeness of the conceptual model. (Measured IQ is known to be highly correlated with SES. This argument further assumes that real innate abilities are also associated with SES.)

Second, when production functions like Eq. 2.2, which includes a measure of "raw inputs" (A_{it*}), are analyzed, a further argument seems reasonable. If initial endowments could be presumed to determine the level of the production function and only indirectly to affect the rate of increase of education, the problem of lack of measures is solved by looking at Eq. 2.2. If endowments only affect the rate of increase through the level of initial ability at some time, A_{it*} in Eq. 2.2 adequately accounts for these effects.[k]

For policy purposes, consideration of affecting educational output through changing initial endowments does not seem too profitable. Even solution of the genetic aspects of the idea would leave such a policy in doubt because of the moral issues involved in an active policy of altering innate abilities. These topics, needless to say, are outside the scope of this book. (However, there is evidence that environmental factors such as inadequate diet may cause retardation.[21] Policies aimed at correcting such environmental difficulties are easily justified and do not need support of an educational production function analysis.)

Recognizing the conceptual desirability of innate abilities does aid in the interpretation of empirical models which don't include such factors. The relationship between background and endowments does change the potential interpretations and policy implications associated with family background. Not including initial endowments (because of data reasons) leads to the influence of families, particularly in models like Eq. 2.1, being overstated in importance since

---

[k]This assumption implies an educational analog to a Markov process in probability. The educational level at any time period can be specified as a function of only the level in the last time period. It is not necessary to know the starting point or initial levels. (I_i).

any measured background characteristics will also be a proxy for initial endowments. Thus, in addition to previous discussions of policy involving family characteristics, a further caution is added; any estimated family background effects could well be overstated. The concept of differing initial endowments also crystallizes the futility of partitioning the effects of different inputs, or finding their relative importance, since actual models will blur some of the input distinctions—particularly with respect to family background.

School Factors $[S_i^{(t)}]$

The logical focus of most policy discussions is the school input vector to the educational process. Compared with other inputs, there is more latitude found within the school vector for the application of alternative policies. Further, the most critical decision problems for school administrators are contained within the school vector.

The general elements of the school vector are teacher characteristics and attitudes, physical characteristics of the school, curriculum, etc. It is not worthwhile to specify these completely at this time since many of the hypotheses are well known. Nevertheless, there remain some conceptual points to be made.

Probably the most crucial analytical notion introduced is that the school inputs *relevant to the individual* should be analyzed. Schools are often large and complex places, the extreme being the comprehensive high school which includes several distinct curricula. A school is made up of a set of buildings, teachers, and courses in which all students may or may not share equally. For example, all people in a college preparatory curriculum might benefit from a good algebra teacher; however, those in the business curriculum in the same school might not receive any input from this algebra teacher.[22] Similar arguments can be made for most aspects of the school. In short, the heterogeneity of school inputs may make measures of school inputs such as the availability of item X or the average of item Y very poor measures of the relevant inputs for any given student.

The requirement that the input vector include elements relevant to the individual student is not unique to the school vector. The same argument pertains to the family vector, the peer vector, and the endowments vector. It is made explicit in this case only because there tends to be confusion on how to define school inputs (or, at least, data problems which often negate proper specification). The heterogeneity of the school inputs received by different individuals is often neglected, a shortcoming in modeling which could have very serious effects on the interpretation of school inputs.

In viewing specific hypotheses, perhaps the most important for analyzing the efficiency of the present system arises from the actions of the schools. Schools purchase graduate education, experience levels of teachers, and classes of different sizes, presumably in the belief that these characteristics have a strong positive effect on achievement. If not, schools are being inefficient.

In looking beyond these ready-made hypotheses, however, several issues must be confronted. These revolve around isolating and measuring relevant attributes of a teacher. Is it possible to decompose a teacher (or a school system) into meaningful characteristics which relate to education? Similar questions arise in all phases of this work since abstract qualities such as warmth or communicative skills are important as family inputs to education. As with the family, it is hoped that a considerable portion of "teaching ability" can be captured by objective measures involving background, education, and attitudes of the teacher. For pragmatic reasons related to data availability and reliability, objective measures are emphasized over subjective measures. Also, since administrators do not explicitly buy warmth but instead a bundle of objective characteristics such as college degrees and experience, there is further justification for downplaying the more qualitative aspects. (These issues are less important, but still relevant, in many policy discussions which involve colder elements of a school such as the efficacy of tracking or effects of reducing class size.)

With school inputs the importance of both quantity and quality of inputs introduces some difficulties. Teachers differ in qualitative ways, but, more than that, students receive different quantities of teachers inputs through differences in class size, days of attendance, classroom attention, and the amount of time spent on teaching and on discipline among teachers. The other vectors are more homogeneous in terms of quantity, and the quantity differences which do exist are more easily measured (for example, by family structure). Indeed, the above should convey the impression that, because of both the vagueness of hypotheses and some analytical/conceptual difficulties, specification complexities tend to be most acute in the case of the school vector.

Finally, in addressing policy alternatives that arise in the school inputs, it is tautological that the inputs must be specified in a manner amenable to policy analysis. Analyzing whether or not red haired teachers should be used instead of brown haired teachers requires explicit introduction of hair color into the model of the educational process; furthermore, merely making the distinction between black haired teachers and all other teachers is insufficient. The point is simple: Each analysis must be tailored to the type and range of policy questions being considered.

Functional Form

Since we have so little guidance on the specification of inputs to the educational process, we can hardly hope to have guidance on the functional form of the relationship of inputs to outputs. There is no theoretically correct function $[g]$ for the production process. Given this, the choice of functions is made, at least initially, on empirical grounds. Certain functional forms (namely linear and multiplicative) tend to be easier to analyze statistically than more complex functions. For initial work they are often used since many functions over small ranges can be approximated by these. Given that functional form is treated as an empirical question, it will be discussed subsequently in that context.

The Conceptual Model

The goal of this discussion has been to explain what kinds of information are useful to the educational decision maker and how he should employ them. In the simplest case there are neat and clean decision rules for the hiring of inputs into the educational process. But the precision of these rules evaporates quickly when the abstract decision rules are introduced to the reality of the educational process.

In the most general terms educational output or achievement can be thought of as a function of family background, peers, innate ability, and school factors. But, these fuzzy concepts take on meaning only when they are defined more precisely. Take, for example, the measurement of educational output. It is easy to identify two major components of output—skills and values. It is more difficult to develop precise measures and to find data relating to these two components. And, while the most desirable measures relate to the student's performance in society, it is often necessary to compromise and use proxy measures which are more readily available. Further data availability frequently imposes constraints upon analysis—forcing the analysis of single dimensions of output. To be sure, it would be optimal to view the development of several outputs and the trade-offs among different dimensions. But, since so little is known about any aspect of the educational process, it seems quite reasonable to analyze partial output measures rather than waiting for a chance, a chance which may be long in coming, to develop a comprehensive view of schools.

As far as inputs are concerned, there is an abundance of hypotheses, but they generally are not well specified. They tend to take a form such as "good teachers are what is needed." The analytical problem posed is twofold. First, the hypotheses about various aspects of the educational process must be drawn together; that is, those relating to family background, peer influences, innate abilities, and school inputs. In much of the education literature the different aspects are analyzed separately. Second, it is necessary to define the specific hypotheses in such a manner that measures of the inputs can be developed and the hypotheses can be tested.

The inputs to the educational process are divided into four basic groups, with policy implications and interest varying among them. For most analyses the center of interest for the decision maker is the input of schools. Second to this is the input of peers, especially in the form of student body characteristics. There is considerably less interest in the influence of families and the effects of different innate abilities. These latter aspects are usually not purchased in the market and are for the most part not under the control of the decision maker.

If the decision maker knows the production function for education, he can make some statements about the efficiency of hiring educational inputs for the achievement of each individual child. While the presence of multiple outputs and nonmarket inputs complicates the analysis, a production function, even in terms of single outputs, can provide useful information for efficiency and general educational policy.

3

Single System, Individual Student Analysis

The remainder of this book is devoted to the reality of schools as seen through statistical analyses of the observed happenings within schools. It navigates through a series of hypotheses about the educational process and about what goes on within elementary schools of this country; it presents some conclusions about school operations; and it provides a basis for making further inferences into educational policy. For these purposes, the story of the educational process will be told in terms of regression models explaining cognitive ability and formal tests of the behavior of parents, teachers, and students.

Through the analyses, which are by necessity less general than would be desired, there is an undercurrent of "how to." The simplified, often cryptic, views of education presented here do not answer all of the questions. They are more of a beginning than an end. Education is a $40 billion industry which has been run almost entirely without benefit of knowledge derived from past successes or failures. A significant part of this and subsequent chapters is demonstrating how information about past school operations can be used within the conceptual framework of the decision rule for school administrators to understand better the educational process and to improve future school operations.

This chapter presents a detailed analysis—call it a demonstration analysis—of the educational process within a single school system. These results—intriguing and suggestive as they may be—require confirmation from other sources and other situations.

Looking at one school district has both advantages and disadvantages. Many hard-to-measure attributes such as curriculum, school organization, community attitudes, and so on are automatically taken care of by looking at one school system since they will be roughly constant for all students. Thus, potential biases from community or system-specific variables which cannot be, or are not, measured are eliminated in such a sample. However, the same arguments can be turned around. By looking at only one system it is difficult to make generalizations about behavior in other systems located in different regions and having different types of organizations. If system-specific attributes were very important, it would not be possible to apply the results of the estimated models to other systems. This implies that generalizing the results calls for expansion of the analysis to other systems. Consistency in different samples would strengthen any results considerably. Such confirmation of results is provided in later chapters where the educational process is viewed across many school systems and many experiences, albeit with poorer data than are used within this chapter.

Focusing attention upon a single system has other advantages. It allows a concentration of effort—in data collection, in modeling, and in interpretation—of sufficient scale to look at more detailed hypotheses about behavior and to begin mapping the boundaries of usefulness for this line of inquiry. Two major shortcomings have persisted in the several past studies of the educational process. First, there has been insufficient data to permit the matching of inputs at the individual level, particularly the matching of individual school inputs, with the other inputs and outputs of the educational process. This has led to either biased or inconclusive results. Second, there has been a lack of historical data on inputs. Even though the conceptual model depicts education as a cumulative process, most past studies have relied upon cross-sectional data containing only contemporaneous information about inputs. These data problems have introduced considerable doubt into the conclusions of past studies.[1] A primary objective of this chapter was to come closer to the conceptual models of chapter 2 than had been done previously, by eliminating these two sources of data error. In particular, data were specified and collected for the sole purpose of looking at the educational process instead of attempting to squeeze data gathered for different purposes into the framework of the conceptual model.

Measuring a School System

The basic data sample was drawn during the summer of 1969 from a relatively large urban school system in California, although the system could have been in a variety of places. The city, populated by roughly 100,000 people, has some employment of its own, but is closely related economically to a larger city nearby. Within the city diverse occupations and incomes are observed as they are in urban settings across the country, but the details aren't necessary at this time.

The school system had 30,000 clients during the 1968-69 school year; this analysis concentrates upon the 2,445 third graders. The combined information of school records, surveys, observations, and interviews provided the picture of the school system which is analyzed here. For all 2,445 third grade students, information on family background, scores on the Stanford Achievement Tests of reading proficiency, and names of teachers (for subsequent merging of student and teacher data) were abstracted from cumulative school records. At the same time, all kindergarten through third grade teachers currently in the system were surveyed using a revised and expanded instrument similar to that used for *Equality of Educational Opportunity (EEO)*. Information was collected on teacher backgrounds and attitudes, and on specific aspects of schooling; and an attempt was made to ascertain their use of time, that is, the division in the classroom between instructional efforts, disciplinary efforts, and administration. Also, a verbal facility test was given each teacher.[2] The details of the different components of the data collection will be developed within the description of the actual modeling and testing efforts.

One of the key elements of this endeavor—both conceptually and empirically—is time. The availability of historical information about students through the linking of students with specific past teachers and classrooms also makes this analysis virtually unique.[a] In order to exploit fully the historical content of the data, the actual analysis proceeded using a subsample of data for whom complete historical information was available.[b] The usable sample totalled 1,061 students, an ample number to observe the separate influences of different inputs to the educational process. (A preponderance of the eliminated students was attributable to incomplete teacher data which, in turn, resulted both from the failure to return the voluntary, self-administered survey by slightly over 10 percent of the second and third grade teachers and from teacher turnover.)

This sample reduction was not performed without a cost. By insisting on complete historical data and by anchoring the data collection to third graders within the school system, no real analysis of the educational effects of student mobility is possible. Students who entered the system after the first grade are eliminated because almost certainly no data will be available on their first grade achievement or perhaps their second grade teachers. Mobile populations, within and between communities, represent special educational problems and deserve serious analysis. Unfortunately, this data collection scheme precludes such an analysis.[3]

For analytical purposes, three different samples were analyzed. As a first step, whites and Mexican-Americans were separated. (The latter was the only minority group represented in this particular school system.) Two reasons, which will be amplified in the course of the discussion, formed the basis for this stratification: (a) the nominal values of the proxies for background inputs do not necessarily have the same meaning for the two groups, and (b) there is no reason to insist on the same model of the educational process for both groups. The ethnic samples were also divided on occupational grounds—fathers in manual, or blue-collar, occupations and nonmanual, or white-collar, occupations. Out of this emerged three samples for analysis: white, manual occupation (515 students); white, nonmanual occupation (323 students); and Mexican-American, manual occupa-

---

[a]There are other samples with longitudinal information—for example, the U.S. Office of Education's Project TALENT or New York State's Quality Measurement Project. But these samples have recorded too little information about school resources to be very useful in looking at educational production functions.

[b]First, individuals were eliminated from the sample if survey data were not available on both their second and third grade teachers. Second, students were eliminated if both first and third grade achievement test scores were not available.

tion (140 students).[c] These students were located in twenty-three separate schools and experienced over a hundred separate teachers in the second and third grades.

Do Teachers Count?

There has probably always been controversy within education. But surely none has been as fundamental and as potentially devastating as the recent controversy among those analyzing education as to whether teachers make a difference in the educational process. This question and challenge arise from interpretation of past empirical work (particularly faulty interpretation of *Equality of Educational Opportunity*) and can be partially tested here. Since our sample experience did not include children without teachers, the only testable hypothesis is whether or not there are differences in teachers that lead to differences in achievement among students. In other words, does it matter which teacher a student has, or are all teachers perfectly substitutable? (Similarly, this is the correct formulation of the hypothesis for other analyses since they were also constrained to observing students with teachers.)

There are two approaches in ascertaining whether productive differences exist in teachers, and both will eventually be followed in the course of this analysis. First, one can attempt to identify the individual components of the bundle of characteristics, such as teaching experience, that make up an individual teacher and to relate these to educational output. Alternatively, one can test the "whole bundle" without decomposing it into more basic components. The latter approach is followed originally, since it is more persuasive in the face of theoretical and measurement problems. That is, simply because one can find no significant relationship between a set of measured characteristics of teachers and output does not mean that teachers do not matter. It only means that one is not very confident that the specific *measured characteristics* have any effect on achievement. There still could be other characteristics, unmeasured, that characterize the productive aspects of teachers. Since we have little information on what precise attributes are important, a logical first step involves testing the bundle of "teacherness" without regard to the specific components.

This test is performed by constructing a series of qualitative or dummy variables, T_{ij}, for each teacher in the sample and applying regression analysis to explain third grade achievement in terms of teachers. If the jth student has the ith teacher, $T_{ij} = 1$ for him and $T_{kj} = 0$, where $k \neq i$. The basic model of third grade achievement analyzed looks like:

---

[c]The decision to stratify will be discussed in terms of formal statistical tests for sample homogeneity in a later section.

These samples are not exhaustive. Children with only mothers or those where no occupation was reported for the fathers were not included. For whites, these groups totaled 36 students; for Mexican-Americans, these groups plus the nonmanual occupation group totaled 47. These samples were too small to study separately, and, thus, they were ignored.

$$A_{3j} = \sum_{i=1}^{n} t_i T_{ij} + aF_j + bA_{2j} + u_j \qquad (3.1)$$

where

A_{3j}	= achievement in third grade of the jth student,
F_j	= 1 if jth student is female; = 0 if male,
A_{2j}	= achievement in second grade of jth student,
u_j	= random error for jth student, and
$t_1, \ldots, t_n, a, b$	= estimated regression coefficients.

The t_i's are thus an estimate of the achievement expected by each student in the ith classroom. Further, it is the expected gain independent of the student's sex and prior (second grade) achievement level. For any individual child who was in a given classroom (i), the model reduces to:

$$A_{3j} = t_i + aF_j + bA_{2j} + u_j \qquad (3.2)$$

In this formulation it is possible to ask whether the individual classroom coefficients are significantly different from each other or whether they are essentially equal. In other words, does model (3.1) do significantly better than model (3.3) in explaining achievement?

$$A_{3j} = c + aF_j + bA_{2j} + u_j \qquad (3.3)$$

where c is a constant for students in all classrooms.

This preliminary test of differential teacher effectiveness was performed within each of the three samples: whites with fathers in a manual occupation; whites with fathers in a nonmanual occupation; and Mexican-Americans with fathers in a manual occupation.[d] In fact six separate tests for differences in the t_i's were performed; each sample generated two separate tests: the gains from second to third grade, as depicted in Eq. 3.1 and the gains from first to second grade (the dependent variable is A_{2j} and one exogenous variable is A_{1j}).

The appropriate statistical test is an F-test which indicates whether or not allowing for teacher differences significantly enhances our ability to predict A_{3j}. The results of these six F-tests for equality of teacher coefficients are depicted in table 3.1. For whites, the F-statistic is consistently large and the hypothesis of no teacher differences is rejected at the 1 percent level. However, for Mexican-Americans it is not possible to reject the hypothesis of no teacher differences at the 10 percent level. In other words, the individual teachers ap-

---

[d]At least two students must have had any given teacher before the student and teacher were included in the analysis. This reduced the sample sizes slightly from those given above.

pears to count for whites of all social strata but not for Mexican-Americans.

(One qualification is needed before any further interpretations are made. Since these students had only one teacher during the year, it is impossible at this stage of the analysis to distinguish between the effects of particular teachers and a classroom composition effect. There are no independent observations of a given teacher with several different classrooms or a given classroom with several different teachers. This problem will be dealt with directly in the next section.)

This analysis suggests that the Mexican-Americans at this lower grade level are not getting much out of school. On the average, they tend to progress at a rate of about one-half grade level per year, or 50 percent of the national average, for reading achievement gains, regardless of which teacher they have. It is possible that the classroom composition exactly offsets teacher differences, or that teachers are matched with Mexican-American classes to equalize gains. However, this seems highly unlikely, since it would be difficult to make such a matching. (Remember that the model analyzes the effects of teachers independent of the entering achievement level. The matching needed to achieve no teacher-classroom effects calls for putting the best teacher-classroom combination with the room of worst "gainers," and so on.) Moreover, since the white children are sensitive to teacher-classroom differences, as indicated by table 3-1, a finding of no differences for Mexican-Americans—when in fact white differences exist—implies that teachers are distributed only in conjunction to the Mexican-Americans in the class. Yet, the proportion of Mexican-Americans ranges from 6 percent to 63 percent in the thirty third grade classrooms that have more than two Mexican-American students. The policy implications of this finding for

Table 3-1
F-Statistics for Null Hypothesis of Uniform Teacher Effects

Sample	F	d. f.[a]	R^2
Third Grade			
White, manual	2.03[b]	(69,426)	.71
White, nonmanual	1.57[b]	(57,247)	.76
Mexican-American, manual	.78[c]	(29,78)	.68
Second Grade			
White, manual	2.96[b]	(55,440)	.68
White, nonmanual	2.39[b]	(48,264)	.71
Mexican-American, manual	1.09[c]	(26,82)	.64

[a]Degrees of freedom.
[b]Statistically significant at the 1 percent level.
[c]Statistically insignificant at the 10 percent level.

Mexican-Americans will be discussed in the concluding section of this chapter.

Efficiency Aspects of Schools

Knowing that teachers are different doesn't take us very far in understanding schools. Perhaps only those who have been studying educational production functions would be surprised to hear that there are differences among teachers. Moreover, to be useful more information about the differences in teachers is needed.

The first step of the analysis of specific teacher-classroom characteristics was to ascertain whether or not the current operations of schools could be considered efficient. This was done by estimating the relationship between the "pay parameters" of teaching experience and graduate education and the gains observed in student achievement. For each of the three samples, a linear regression model was estimated with the dependent variable being third grade achievement and the independent variables being first grade achievement, characteristics of the family and classroom, and years of teaching experience (EXPER) and semester hours of graduate work (UNITS) for each student's specific second and third grade teacher.[e] From this it is possible to test the hypothesis that the pay parameters do not affect the learning of children. If the pay parameters were to affect learning, it would also be possible to ascertain whether the pay scale correctly reflected the educational value of each element; that is, the marginal product of say a year's experience could be compared with the price of a year's experience.

The results of the hypothesis tests for each sample are shown in table 3-2. This table displays the t-statistic values for tests of the hypothesis that the individual pay parameters for the second and third grade teachers have no effect on the achievement gains of individual students. As evidenced by the very low values of the t-statistics, we cannot reject the hypothesis that the factors purchased by schools have no effect on this measure of output.[f] In fact, only five of the twelve estimated coefficients are larger than their standard errors ($t > 1.0$), and one of those has a conceptually incorrect sign.

In other words, we are not very confident that any of the attributes of teachers that are explicitly purchased have any effect on education. Schools are, seemingly, paying too much for the amount contributed by these attributes to education if they buy any quantity above the minimum level. (This is an overstatement if turnover costs are large.)

However, the above results still give minimum guidance to an administrator.

---

[e] In order to calculate semester hours of graduate work, a master's degree was assumed to be 30 semester hours.

[f] If $|t| < 1.96$, the hypothesis of no effect at the 5 percent level cannot be rejected.

Table 3-2
Tests for Significant Effect of Pay Parameters

	t-statistics		
Variable	White Manual	White Nonmanual	Mex.-Amer. Manual
$EXPER_3$	.58	1.16	−.45
$UNITS_3$	.82	.06	1.62
$EXPER_2$	−.75	.19	1.45
$UNITS_2$	1.23	.07	−1.62

Note: Complete Model: $Achievement_3$ = f(sex, income, siblings, number of absences, percentage Mexican-American in school, average income in school, $Achievement_1$, $EXPER_3$, $UNITS_3$, $EXPER_2$, $UNITS_2$) where subscripts indicate grade level of student or teacher and a linear equation is estimated. EXPER is total teaching experience in years, and UNITS is semester hours past a bachelor's degree.

While they indicate what he should not do, they give an imperfect picture of what he should do. For his purposes we wish to identify what attributes of teachers do seem to count. That is the emphasis of the remainder of this chapter.

Characteristics of Teachers

The preceding section suggested that the performance of white students is dependent upon the specific teacher and classroom associated with the student. For policy purposes it would be useful to identify the characteristics that contribute to increased performance. This phase of the analysis was accomplished by introducing a variety of quantitative teacher and classroom characteristics into an overall model of student achievement.[g] This was done for both the white manual occupation and white nonmanual occupation samples.

Within an area such as education, where very little is known about the educational production process, a certain amount of experimentation with model specification is both necessary and desirable. There are a plethora of hypotheses about the educational process—everyone has his favorite. An attempt was made to test as many of the major hypotheses as possible given the data

[g]An intuitively appealing analysis of teacher characteristics calls for estimating value added models which use the estimated coefficients, t_i, from Eq. 3.1 as the dependent variable and characteristics of just the teachers and classrooms for the independent variables. However, there are some very severe statistical problems with this. In particular, the usual ordinary least squares assumption that the error variance-covariance matrix is $\sigma^2 I$ is untenable. If we let the variance-covariance matrix of estimated coefficients from Eq. 3.1 equals Ω and assume that value added is stochastic with an error matrix of $\sigma^2 I$, then the error matrix in estimating a value added would be $(\Omega + \sigma^2 I)$ where σ^2 is unknown. An efficient estimator requires a two step estimation procedure such as the one suggested in Eric A. Hanushek, "Efficient Estimators for Regressing Regression Coefficients," (mimeo), 1971.

limitations, but, since many of the hypotheses are vague and ill-defined, it is very difficult to provide conclusive tests.

The models presented in this and subsequent chapters are the most promising ones of the educational process and were selected through the informal application of two criteria: (1) conformity with a priori views about the process, and (2) statistical properties of the estimated models, chiefly significance of individual parameters. These two criteria were never in serious conflict.

White, Manual Occupation

The estimates for the white manual sample are displayed in Eq. 3.4. Variables definitions, means, and standard deviations appear in table 3-3.

$$A_3 = 20.8 + 2.81F - 6.38R + .79A_1 - .07D \qquad (3.4)$$
$$(2.3) \quad (-2.8) \quad (18.8) \quad (-2.1)$$
$$+ .09T_3 - .57Y_3 + .06T_2 - .68Y_2$$
$$(2.4) \quad (-1.5) \quad (1.9) \quad (-2.9)$$
$$R^2 = .51 \qquad\qquad SE = 13.5$$

Table 3-3
Variable Definitions, Means and Standard Deviations — White Manual Occupation Model

Variable	Mean	Standard Deviation	Definition
A_3	55.74	19.1	Stanford Achievement Test raw score—third grade
F	.50	.5	Sex: = 1 for female = 0 for male
R	.08	.3	Repeat grade: = 1 if a grade was repeated; = 0 otherwise
A_1	35.17	15.1	Stanford Achievement Test raw score—first grade
D	17.93	18.8	Percentage of time spent on discipline by third grade teacher
T_3	66.90	15.8	*Quick Word Test* score—third grade teacher
Y_3	1.91	1.6	Years since most recent educational experience—third grade teacher
T_2	68.41	19.0	*Quick Word Test* score—second grade teacher
Y_2	2.64	2.6	Years since most recent educational experience—second grade teacher

(*t*-statistics are displayed below each coefficient; *SE* is the standard error of estimate. Subscripts indicating individuals *(j)* have been omitted for notational simplicity.)

While no variable in the model explicitly relates to family backgrounds, the influence of families is not absent. The data have been stratified on the basis of father's occupation. Thus, family influences can be seen by looking at differences between this model and the one estimated for children from nonmanual occupation families. This way of looking at families—sample stratification—was not the only way analyzed. Within the stratified samples, dummy variables for basic occupational differences, for example foreman and skilled craftsman or laborer, were analyzed but added little to the explanation of student achievement. Also, occupational categories were converted to a continuous income measure (using median incomes from Census data), but proved to be of little value in identifying educational differences. It is worthwhile noting, however, that the estimated coefficients for school factors were quite insensitive to the precise specification of family inputs.

Before going into the measurement of schools and teachers, a word about the individual characteristic variables, F and R, is appropriate. As has been noted by others in the past, females (particularly at an early age) perform better than males.[4] On average, third grade girls do 2.8 points better than boys. Further, if we know the student has already repeated a grade, we expect a considerably poorer performance from the student, everything else equal. This is not very surprising.

This model presents an interesting view of teachers. The teacher characteristics that appear to be important are not the characteristics that are purchased by schools. For both the second and third grade teachers, the score on the verbal facility test *(T)* and the recentness of education *(Y)* are the most important factors.[h] Additionally, there is a "quasi-teacher" characteristic—the percentage of time spent on discipline by the third grade teacher. Each of these has important implications for school operations.

The verbal facility test *(T)* probably proxies two attributes of teachers. First, it is a measure of communicative ability of the teacher. Second, as the authors of the test point out, it can be taken as a quick measure of overall intelligence or general ability. The logic of this latter factor is obvious—more intelligent teachers can express concepts in more different ways, can draw ideas together better, can identify student needs more easily, etc. Interestingly, this picture of education indicates that general ability seems important, regardless of formal training.

There are some important policy implications surrounding differences in this

---

[h]The model was not constrained to have the same characteristics for second and third grade teachers; this results from the analysis of various characteristics without constraint. If we test the joint hypotheses that all four strictly-teacher characteristics together have no effect on education, we reject at the .01 level with $F_{4,506} = 5.68$.

measure of teacher quality. Differences in teacher abilities can have a powerful effect on student achievement. By interchanging teachers at the top and bottom of the verbal ability scale within this system, mean student reading achievement changes by .2 to .4 grade levels.[i] This range of achievement levels is significant at early grades. Past studies have suggested increasing grade level disparities, implying that deviations from expected educational development which occur in early years will be magnified in subsequent years.[5] Within this analysis, the powerful effect of the student's early education on later achievement is also evident. The strength of first grade achievement in Eq. 3.4 is impressive; a 1 percent lower first grade score implies, ceteris paribus a 1¼ percent lower third grade score.[j] Thus, the teacher distribution according to verbal facility score can have an important and lasting effect on individual children.

Since this test has national norms, it is possible to get some idea of how the teachers being hired in this system rate alongside other college graduates. The mean system score of 68 places the teachers in this sample slightly under the median for female college graduates. Thus, this system is not being successful in attracting the best people—a point we will return to soon.

In addition to teacher ability as measured by the verbal facility test, the recentness of educational experiences (Y) has a significant effect on educating students. The more recent the teacher's educational experiences, the better her students' performance is. This provides a rationale for encouraging or requiring teachers to take additional courses periodically. However, as indicated by the results of analyzing graduate units and the effects of master's degrees, it does not really matter whether the teacher is enrolled in an advanced degree program or, for that matter, taking many courses. Education of a student's second and third grade teachers in the past year as opposed to five years ago would, on average, be worth .2 to .3 years of reading achievement to the student.

Finally, there is the measure of discipline time (D) that was labeled as a quasi-teacher characteristic. Certainly, an interaction between the classroom and the teacher is reflected in this variable, and, thus, this cannot be considered to be strictly a teacher measure or strictly a student measure. As would be expected, the more time spent on disciplinary matters, the lower the achievement level of

---

[i]This is calculated by changing only the third grade teacher verbal score for the lower limit and both second and third for the upper limit. The scores are changed from 40 to 96 to represent the range found in the data (maximum score is 100). The resulting achievement score is then converted to grade level equivalents.

[j]These calculations apply for deviations from the first and third grade mean achievement levels. This is actually the first of many times in which the concept of *elasticity* will be used in this book. Elasticity, a unit free number, indicates what percentage change can be expected from a one percent change in a given independent variable. In a linear model, such as Eq. 3.4, the elasticity will be different according to the magnitude of the independent and dependent variable. The figure given in the text refers to the means of the two variables and is calculated according to the general formula: elasticity = $b(\overline{X}/\overline{Y})$ where b is the linear regression coefficient, $\overline{X}$ is the mean of the particular independent variable, and $\overline{Y}$ is the mean of the dependent variable.

the class. This does suggest that, regardless of the source of interruptions for disciplinary reasons, efforts to reduce such time could be beneficial. Obvious suggestions include using principals or assistant principals or even teacher's helpers as disciplinarians and adjusting classroom compositions to minimize "critical masses" of disciplinary problems.

Let us, within the context of this estimated production function, reconsider the hiring process. It is obvious that the productive factors are not the characteristics of teachers that are currently being purchased. Even within the current salary structure, if there is an excess supply of teachers, schools can attempt to evaluate the general ability of teachers and can be selective in hiring. However, casual observation suggests that past attempts at being "selective" may have been misguided; for example, the most selective (suburban) systems appear to have historically weighted previous teaching experience heavily. Moreover, as confirmed by the simple correlation matrix for teacher characteristics displayed in table 3-4, the purchased factors (experience and units of graduate work) are not highly correlated with the productive characteristics included in the model.

White, Nonmanual Occupation

The estimated model for the white nonmanual student population provides some contrast.[k] The results of this analysis, shown in Eq. 3.5, provided a different set of teacher characteristics that seemed important.

$$A_3 = 35.0 + .72A_1 - 5.1C - .79Y_3 + .10S_3 - .66Y_2 + .20S_2$$
$$(16.0) \quad (-3.0) \quad (-1.9) \quad (1.2) \quad (-1.7) \quad (1.8)$$

$$R^2 = .52 \qquad SE = 11.8 \qquad\qquad (3.5)$$

Variable definitions, means and standard deviations are displayed in table 3-5. In comparison with the manual occupation model, the coefficient estimates are not as reliable in the nonmanual sample. Although there is a smaller standard error

---

[k]A word on sample stratification is necessary. A formal covariance test for equality of coefficients between the two white models was performed. The methodology of this test can be found in Franklin M. Fisher, "Tests of Equality Between Sets of Coefficients in Two Linear Regressions: An Expository Note," *Econometrica*, March 1970. When testing the entire model and restricting the models for both samples to the form of Eq. 3.4, the hypothesis of coefficient equality was rejected at the .025 level ($F_{9,820} = 2.13$). However, since the principal interest centers upon teacher characteristics, a test of this subset of variables alone seems more appropriate. When this test is performed, the results are inconclusive, since $F_{4,820} = 1.57$ when the critical value for those degrees of freedom at the .10 level is 1.94. Thus, it is not possible to reject the hypothesis of homogeneity with a high level of confidence; yet, at the same time, the evidence does not seem strong enough to pool the sample. Since both samples are large, the loss in efficiency by not pooling would not be large, and the decision was made to stratify.

Table 3-4
Simple Correlations for Teacher Characteristics—White Manual Sample

	D	T_3	Y_3	T_2	Y_2	$EXPER_3$	$UNITS_3$	$EXPER_2$	$UNITS_2$
D	1.00								
T_3	−.19	1.00							
Y_3	.01	.08	1.00						
T_2	.07	.19	.13	1.00					
Y_2	−.14	−.09	.11	−.19	1.00				
$EXPER_3$	−.14	.37	.11	.17	.05	1.00			
$UNITS_3$	−.09	.01	−.14	.09	.12	.53	1.00		
$EXPER_2$	.09	−.11	−.01	−.09	.20	−.18	−.11	1.00	
$UNITS_2$	−.02	.07	.01	−.03	−.15	−.02	.03	.43	1.00

Table 3-5
Variable Definitions, Means and Standard Deviations—White Nonmanual Occupation Model

Variable	Mean	Standard Deviation	Definition
A_3	64.82	16.8	Stanford Achievement Test raw score— third grade
A_1	42.43	15.8	Stanford Achievement Test raw score— first grade
C	.19	.4	Clerical occupation: = 1 if father in clerical job; = 0 otherwise
Y_3	2.02	1.7	Years since most recent educational experience—third grade teacher
S_3	7.85	8.1	Years of experience with this socio-economic level—third grade teacher
Y_2	1.88	1.7	Years since most recent educational experience—second grade teacher
S_2	7.94	6.1	Years of experience with this socio-economic level—second grade teacher

of estimate for the nonmanual model, this is coupled with a smaller variance in overall achievement; the R^2's in the two models are almost equal.

Within the nonmanual occupation sample, there is some heterogeneity in family educational inputs; children from families with clerical jobs perform consistently poorer than children from managerial, professional, technical, or sales occupation families. (Similar tests for differences in family inputs within the manual occupation sample were also performed, but no differences were found.) Within this sample, initial achievement was again important (with an elasticity at the mean achievement level of 1.1), but there were no significant differences between girls and boys.

In the white, nonmanual model the recentness of education is again a significant factor, with approximately the same effect here as in the previous model. However, teacher verbal ability does not appear to be significant. Instead, experience with this socioeconomic group assumes importance. As would be expected, the correlation between total experience and socioeconomic group experience is quite high; the simple correlation for third grade teachers is .8. Thus, the present policies of paying a bonus for experience is more reasonable in this case because some gains in achievement can be related, albeit indirectly, to the purchased input. It is likely though that the experience bonus is too much in an economic efficiency sense. Recentness of education is only slightly correlated with the pay factors, as in the manual occupation sample.

The estimated coefficients in Eq. 3.5 hint that teachers have less effect on these nonmanual children. Although the effects of recent education are roughly the same in the two models, the potential for change in achievement through increasing teacher verbal facility, or general ability, is considerably greater than the potential implied by socioeconomic experience. Not only can verbal facility be changed more rapidly—since experience usually comes by aging rather than hiring—but also given percentage changes in verbal quality have a considerably larger effect on student achievement.

Another way of viewing this is that school quality is not as important for students from higher socioeconomic backgrounds as it is for students from poorer backgrounds. The education in the homes of children from white-collar families apparently insulates these children from variances in teacher quality, at least considerably more than the outside school experiences of children from blue-collar families. Moreover, this education in the home is sufficient to insure that white-collar children have a mean achievement significantly higher than that of either blue-collar whites or Mexican-Americans.

Inconsequential Inputs

The previous discussions of Eqs. 3.4 and 3.5 must be taken within the context of the overall analysis. The survey data contain a much richer picture of teachers and students than finally appeared in the estimated production function. The final models were not, however, the result of arbitrary or capricious decisions in analysis. In the process of developing these models, several other extremely important hypotheses about the educational process were tested and discarded. The tableau of these is a valuable ingredient in concocting a coherent picture of the educational process.

The most notable absent factor in the models is any measure of peer influences or the composition of schools and classrooms. Classroom and school composition are at the forefront of many discussions of education—and are the subject of a subsequent chapter in this book. Certainly the issues—neighborhood schools, ability grouping, busing, etc.—cannot be treated lightly; at this point, however, the range of hypotheses and methods of analysis will be presented without discussion of the policy implications. Three basic ways of viewing classroom compositions were delineated: ethnic composition, socioeconomic composition, and ability composition. The data used here are probably the best ever available for these purposes, since students can be identified by classroom. Nevertheless, the universal finding was that no group was significantly affected, positively or negatively, by school or classroom composition. For each school and classroom, the percentage of students who were Mexican-American and who were in manual occupation families proved insignificant, as did the mean and variance of first grade achievement for the whole class and for each ethnic/occupation group in each classroom.

At the same time variables measuring the student's health and family structure; variables measuring objective background characteristics of the teachers, such as socioeconomic background, college major, and membership in professional organizations; and variables measuring subjective factors, such as attitudes toward types of students, were tested and found to exhibit statistically insignificant effects on the students' achievement. Additionally, the combination of organizational and management skills of the principal and school facility differences were tested by allowing different school-specific intercepts in Eqs. 3.4 and 3.5; the hypothesis of no difference among schools could not be rejected. Further, the possibility that high and low achievers obeyed different production functions was analyzed. The samples were stratified on the basis of above or below mean performance on the first grade exam; no significant differences were found between high and low achievers.

Finally, to round out the discussion, there were a number of interesting hypotheses which could not be tested with these data. The uniformity of class size (within one or two students of twenty-eight pupils/teacher), of curriculum, and of textbooks prevented any examination of these factors. The availability of only one output measure—reading achievement—also restricted the scope of the analysis to cognitive development. But without going further in listing what cannot be analyzed, most of which is quite obvious, it is more profitable to turn to what has been learned.

Single System Conclusions

From this analysis three conclusions are apparent. It should be borne in mind that these conclusions derive from a sample of one school system: therefore, some caution should be used in generalizing to other systems.

An Efficient System. The present set of hiring practices leads to an inefficient allocation of resources. The analysis indicates that teaching experience and graduate education do not contribute to gains in student achievement scores. Moreover, the characteristics that do matter are not highly correlated with these factors. Yet, teaching experience and advanced degrees continue to be purchased by the school district. Since turnover is costly, some average experience level over one year would be reasonable. Nevertheless, the current average of over eleven years is certainly excessive, and, in fact, a rough estimate of the extra costs of incorrect hiring can be made. The distribution of the 236 sampled first through third grade teachers by teaching experience and academic credits beyond a bachelor's degree can be matched with the 1968-69 salary structure for the school system analyzed. From this, an estimate can be made of the salary overpayments, in the sense of payments for nonproductive inputs. If the school hired teachers with just a bachelor's degree and less than two years experience, a savings of 22 percent from present salary payments could be realized. From the models developed this savings would not be accompanied by a drop in achievement.

This opens up several interesting policy alternatives. One distinct possibility would be simply to increase teacher turnover in order to reduce the total wage bill. However, a more appealing policy might be to increase the base salary level in an attempt to attract generally more qualified teachers. (More qualified, again, is not the traditional statement in terms of experience and graduate experience; instead it is related to student learning.) It could be possible to change the composition of the teacher pool through such a change in entry salaries.

At the same time, since a completely flat salary schedule has its own built-in disincentives, a system of pay raises based upon student outputs could be introduced. The mechanism for such a system is the one developed here. Through the estimation procedure displayed, it is possible to estimate the value added by a teacher. The estimated coefficients (t_i) in Eq. 3.1 are estimates of the additions to output added by each teacher. Further, these are additions which are independent of entering achievement and social class background of the student. This is just what is needed to assess the value of individual teachers.

The introduction of such a system would not be easy. There are a host of problems involving measurement of outputs, the politics of introducing such a system (obviously many present teachers could lose under such a system), and so forth. However, it is inconceivable that a system geared to present accomplishments rather than past accomplishments will not be introduced. This is an operational form of *accountability*, a concept which is now just a slogan, but which appears to be gaining broad-based support.

Changing the pay schedule to one with higher entry levels and increases based upon abilities could bring some dramatic changes. The models presented indicated that sizable changes can be made in achievement for any individual student by shuffling the present group of teachers. A change in the salary structure for teachers could change the composition of the pool of available teachers. Certainly within a single system, the pool could be changed through bidding teachers away from other systems. However, changing the entire structure could elevate the quality of teachers nationwide.

Mexican-American Education. In the sense that different teachers and different classroom compositions do not affect the achievement outcome of Mexican-American students, teachers do not appear to count for this group. For Mexican-Americans from blue-collar families, once the entering achievement level is known, no other information is useful in predicting the achievement level after a given year of school. Further, the average gains in a given school year are about one-half of the national average for reading achievement gains; that is, their reading achievement advances about one-half year in each of the second and third grades.

There has been evidence that blacks are more responsive to teachers than whites.[1] The insensitivity of Mexican-Americans to teacher differences, then, may well be a language problem and not just a minority problem: (No direct measure of language in the home is included in the study.) It is worth noting that there are no Mexican-American teachers in this sample. Therefore, there is no test of one of the most prominent policy recommendations, that of hiring teachers who understand the problems of the Mexican-American student from personal experience. The empirical evidence in this study supplies no immediate remedy for this problem.

Given the range of classroom composition, desegregation does not appear to be the answer for the raising achievement of this population. A range of alternatives from English as a second language to community control has been presented in other locales, but these cannot be evaluated in the context of the district sampled in this study.

The record for Mexican-Americans in California and the Southwestern states has not been good. Much of this has been traced to the language problem. As stated by an educational psychologist involved with California Chicanos,

We know all the Spanish-speaking children, close to 60 percent, coming to schools have problems in speaking English because their bilingual background interferes with the ability to communicate and learn. Yet, the only tools that our teachers have to teach them in English is to teach vocabulary. The sound and structure of the English language the teachers don't know how to teach.[6]

One result is that a disproportionate number of Spanish-surname children are labeled mentally retarded and funneled into special classes when in fact they are not retarded in a mental ability sense.[7] They may, however, be retarded in a schooling sense if required to speak, learn and think in English.

If school systems are not providing the special services needed to deal with the particular problems of one population, the arguments for community control of the schools are much more compelling. This is the exact situation confronted by calls for community control.[8]

Measuring Teacher Differences. Differences in teachers and classrooms do make a difference to white children, regardless of their socioeconomic level. There are

---

[1]See chapters 4 and 5, below.

significant differences in the performance of white children, depending upon what classroom they are in. These differences in gains are independent of their entering achievement level, their socioeconomic status, and their sex. And, in order to provide more information, an attempt was made to decompose the estimated gains associated with given teachers and classrooms.

The attempts to develop a set of measurable characteristics that schools could use in hiring and administration to affect achievement did not produce clear-cut answers. A considerable part of teaching cannot be explained by a set of standard variables measuring teachers and classrooms, particularly for white students from white-collar families.

Thus, at least for the present, it is difficult to devise good rules to use in hiring. The characteristics which can be used to predict good teaching performance continue to elude us. However, as discussed in the plans for altering the teacher salary schedules, it is possible to judge how well a teacher did during the year. After the fact, there are good decision rules available. And this may be sufficient to develop considerably improved school systems.

Nevertheless, it would be imprudent to generalize from these findings. They refer to one school system and one particular grade level in elementary schools. For this reason, this study is best looked upon as being suggestive rather than definitive, as being a prototype rather than a final analysis. Replication of this type of individual analysis in many different situations is called for. This means looking at different grade levels, different time spans, and different districts. The next two chapters provide part of this replication through analysis of sixth grade achievement over many school districts, albeit for poorer data.

4

Multisystem Analysis — White Education

The single school system analysis in chapter 3 is quite suggestive and is useful in answering some of the basic education questions now before us. Yet, given the admonitions pertaining to the single system character of the data, it would be useful to ascertain whether or not these findings can be confirmed in other samples and analyses.

Wider support is forthcoming from an analysis of Office of Education survey data for 1965. In particular, the data which were collected for *Equality of Educational Opportunity*, or the *Coleman Report*, were re-analyzed within the conceptual framework described in chapter 2. One subset of the data in this national survey (referred to subsequently as the *OE Survey*) was examined in depth in order to investigate the same questions asked in the single system analysis. Separate analyses for whites and blacks in the sixth grade in the urban Northeast and Great Lakes regions were performed. The results are quite similar to the previous results: teachers do perform an important role, but the characteristics of teachers which are important are not necessarily those which are purchased by schools.

This analysis has its own ambiguities due to significant data problems. The data are not as good as those for the single system analysis.[a] For this reason, the basic conceptual model must be modified. The next section discusses the model modifications and the sample of data used. A more complete description of the problems associated with the *OE Survey* can be found in the Appendix.

Separate production functions for whites and blacks are estimated. While there are many similarities in the models, this chapter discusses only the education of whites. Discussion of the education of blacks is reserved for chapter 5.

Model Modification and Sample Data

The models of education in this and the following chapter have many similarities in approach and interpretation to the models in chapter 3. But there are also some important differences. To begin with, the models here rely entirely upon cross-sectional data—data with little historical information. While not having accurate historical information about inputs affects all of the inputs and, thus,

---

[a]The single system data were collected after the *OE Survey* data and thus capitalized on the previous experiences of the *OE Survey*.

estimated coefficients, it has its largest impact upon the precise form of the estimated model. In particular, since the data do not contain past achievement scores, the "value-added" form of the educational process depicted in Eq. 2.2 cannot be used. Instead, one must rely upon the complete history model in Eq. 2.1.

This is one of the most compelling reasons for analyzing elementary schools. As time goes on, unraveling the interlaced inputs to the educational process generally becomes more difficult; if an incomplete history of inputs must be relied upon, say by high school, it becomes virtually impossible to distinguish among the contributions of each. Therefore, on top of the general arguments about the importance of early education and simplicity of elementary school organization, this particular data set almost requires focusing exclusive attention upon elementary schools.[b]

A second divergence between the models of this chapter and those of the previous one relates to the unit of analysis. Instead of estimating the individual relationships depicted by Eq. 2.1, a "school" production function is analyzed. In other words, schools—not individuals—are used as the basic observational unit in the statistical analysis, and aggregate school characteristics are substituted for the individual characteristics in the conceptual model.

While the use of individuals certainly would be preferable, the data will not support such a procedure. The major reason for using a school model is the lack of information about school inputs for the individual student. The *OE Survey* included data on individual achievement and socioeconomic background, but it did not include information on individual school inputs. The errors in measurement introduced at the individual level by this failing would surely lead to considerable bias in any statistical estimates of individual models of the production process.

Problems of nonresponse and faulty response also suggest the use of school production functions. Many of the key individual socioeconomic questions such as parental education, are subject to considerable nonresponse. If estimation were done at the individual level, this problem could introduce severe biases since the evidence indicates that much of the nonresponse was systematic (by race and social class). While nonresponse will cause problems at any level of estimation, it is less severe at the school level. At least for elementary schools the general consistency of neighborhood composition (with the prevalence of neighborhood attendance districts) insures that any missing observations will not affect the school aggregates by very much.[c] Similarly, faulty response will not

---

[b]There is a trade-off in the *OE Survey* data. The basic sample gathered information on first and third graders, and analysis of either would reduce the time dimension from the chosen sixth grade study. However, the data for earlier grades were fewer and less accurate. The achievement tests in the third grade were additionally subject to difficulties relating to "topping out"; that is, it was relatively easy to get a perfect score.

[c]In a formal statistical sense, the concern centers upon the size of the variance in measurement errors relative to the variance in the true variable. Compared with the individual variables, the errors at the school level are almost certainly less severe.

have an overpowering influence at the school level. The pervasiveness of these data problems provides considerable support for the position that any production functions using *OE Survey* data must be estimated at the school level.

The *OE Survey* included four separate cognitive development tests at the sixth grade: verbal ability, nonverbal ability, mathematics achievement, and reading achievement. The verbal ability test was the Educational Testing Service's School and College Ability Test (SCAT); nonverbal ability was the Inter-American Test; reading and mathematics achievement were ETS Sequential Tests of Educational Progress (STEP). There is no clear decision rule for choosing among these tests to arrive at a measure of educational output.

The difference in scope of the ability and achievement tests provides one consideration in the choice of output measure. Ability tests have been designed to measure learning capacity or IQ; achievement tests on the other hand are concerned with specific subject matter. However, there has been considerable recent evidence suggesting that such distinctions are not meaningful.[1] While few people now consider ability tests as anything more than broader achievement tests, it is this difference in scope that is meaningful in formulating an output scale.[2] If ability tests cover a different scope than achievement tests, it is useful to evaluate differences in school impact in producing each.

Prior beliefs about components of the process when measured in different directions offer a second guide in selection of a specific output measure. Intuitively, it seems that measures of verbal factors would be more closely linked to home environment and, thus, harder for schools to affect than other possible measures. The main source of verbal instruction is the home; children are constantly under the influence of the speech patterns of the family. The school either refines the basics learned elsewhere or attempts the much more tedious job of overthrowing incorrect verbal patterns introduced outside of the school, a job at which the last chapter indicated schools are not always successful. Which job the school undertakes depends on the quality of the student's background. On the other hand, schools could seemingly be operated much more independently in areas less tied to nonschool influences, e.g., "new" math. This implies that schools could have a differential impact on output measured in different directions. A priori the impact of schools would be less in the case of verbal ability than in the case of the other output measures.

While these considerations do not make a strong case for selecting a particular measure of output, they do provide motivation for analyzing more than one. In order to test the two inter-output hypotheses about school effects, two separate production functions were estimated: one for verbal ability, and one for mathematics achievement. Verbal ability was chosen as verbal skills appear to be highly rewarded in hiring and advancements. Additionally, most subsequent analyses of the *OE Survey* data center on the production of these verbal skills.[3] Math then provides the comparison of measures.

The white production functions were estimated from a sample of 471 elementary schools. These are all *OE Survey* schools with complete information and more than four white sixth graders found in standard metropolitan statistical areas (SMSAs) in a geographic region covering the New England, Mid-Atlantic, and Great Lakes states.[d]

This region was chosen on the basis of relevance to educational policy and an a priori view that it was relatively homogeneous in terms of culture and attitudes. The major reason for stratification of the *OE Survey* schools is a concern over homogeneity, although the issue of data manageability does enter. If the observations are not part of the same population (i.e., do not follow the same behavioral relationships), the estimated production functions will be meaningless. It seems plausible that rural schools operate under a different production process due to different organizational structures, size considerations, variations in parental attitudes, and the impact of socioeconomic standards, etc. There is also some empirical verification for the assertion that there are urban-rural differences found in Kiesling's study.[4] Even so, this division is not too critical in terms of making inferences about the population as 78 percent of the people in the sample region reside in urban places.[5]

Homogeneity considerations also entered into restriction of the sample to the North region. Different characteristics of the various regions of the country in terms of attitudes, support of schools, cultural influences, etc., suggest stratification for the production function estimation. The *OE Survey* itself provides information about the considerable differences in both inputs and outputs in different regions of the country. While this does not establish the necessity of stratification, the magnitude of these differences plus prior knowledge about differences in social climate, economic conditions, and migration patterns afford prima facie evidence for this procedure.[e] While it would be desirable for policy purposes to have a complete picture of education in all sections, the magnitude of such an undertaking forced selection of one region for this study. As mentioned previously, the North was chosen as this is the center of much of the current controversy over education. This is especially true when one considers differences in education by race.

In forming the sample, all schools with four or less white sixth graders were eliminated. This arbitrary cutoff point was established to insure that the admonitions about individual production functions were not violated. The effect

---

[d]SMSAs follow the Bureau of the Census definitions used in the 1960 *Census of Population.* SMSAs follow county boundaries and include contiguous counties to a county containing a city of 50,000 or more people.

The states included in the sample along with their number of sample schools are: Connecticut (24), Delaware (6), Illinois (28), Indiana (35), Maine (10), Maryland (13), Massachusetts (42), Michigan (51), New Hampshire (0), New Jersey (36), New York (89), Ohio (22), Pennsylvania (64), Rhode Island (0), Vermont (0), Washington, D.C. (2), and Wisconsin (49).

[e]The tremendous regional differences, especially North-South differences, are well documented in chapter 2 of *EEO.*

of this sampling decision was to eliminate 57 schools which contained one to four white sixth graders. This drastically reduced the number of observations of schools with high concentrations of blacks and other minorities. However, reduction in range of some characteristics seems more than compensated for by the reduction in errors of the explanatory variables.

After the elimination of "small schools,"[f] there are still observations across the entire range of black-white composition, but, as table 4-1 displays, the distribution drops off sharply.[g] Of the 471 white schools in the sample, 169 schools have five or more black sixth graders. Even so, this sample does not belie the true situation in public schools. The extent of racial concentrations within school systems is described extensively in the Civil Rights Commission Report, *Racial Isolation in the Public Schools.*[6] In a sample of 75 school systems from the entire country reported in *Racial Isolation,* 83 percent of the white elementary students attended schools with over 90 percent white. (At the same time, 75 percent of the black elementary students attended schools which were over 90 percent black.) Thus, while there are some overall questions about the representativeness of the sampled schools, in these aggregate terms the sample seems reasonable.

Of the sampled schools half are located in central cities. In size they range from 5 to 160 white sixth graders. The average total number of sixth graders in the sampled schools is 72 and the average total school size is 600. (This latter figure is somewhat misleading for the sampled schools vary widely in grade composition.)

Background variables for the student body are defined only over the subset of white students; the characteristics of black and other minority do not enter in computing socioeconomic variables and attitude variables for the "school." Thus, while there are integrated schools in the sample, the 471 schools with over four whites will be referred to as the "white school sample." Similarly, the black production functions in chapter 5 are estimated from a sample of 242 "black schools" even though 169 of these are also in the white school sample.

Table 4-1
Distribution of White Schools by Percentage of Sixth Graders Who Are Black

					Percentage Black					
	None	0-10	10-20	20-30	30-40	40-50	50-60	60-70	70-80	80-90	90-100
No. of Schools	157	158	46	27	30	12	17	10	8	5	1
Percentage	33	33	10	6	6	3	4	2	2	1	0

---

[f]Small here applies to the number of whites, not the total school population.
[g]The figure does misrepresent the composition of schools to the extent that other minorities are present. For whites the proportion of all minorities seems more relevant.

Educational Production Functions for White Sixth Graders

Estimated educational production functions for white sixth graders are presented in Eqs. 4.1 and 4.2.

$$VERBAL* = -1.18 - .023CC + .618G* + .169E_f^* - .064FS*$$
$$(-3.0) \quad (-3.8) \quad (10.6) \quad (6.0) \quad (-2.3)$$

$$+ .004NS* - .006M* + .290HS* - .026S*$$
$$(2.3) \quad (-2.0) \quad (4.4) \quad (-5.6)$$

$$+ .125T* + .019E* - .023NT* - .037N_{75-100}^*$$
$$(2.4) \quad (3.0) \quad (-6.8) \quad (-3.4)$$

$$R^2 = .78 \qquad SE = .38 \qquad\qquad (4.1)$$

$$MATH* = -1.84 - .022CC + .471G* + .225E_f^* - .119FS*$$
$$(-4.3) \quad (-2.8) \quad (6.3) \quad (6.4) \quad (-3.3)$$

$$+ .003NS* - .009M* + .419HS* - .033S*$$
$$(1.6) \quad (-2.2) \quad (6.8) \quad (-5.6)$$

$$+ .089T* + .016E* - .020NT*$$
$$(1.3) \quad (2.1) \quad (-4.6)$$

$$SE = .49 \qquad\qquad (4.2)$$

*Asterisks denote logarithms of variables. t-statistics are displayed in parentheses below each coefficient. SE is the standard error of the weighted regression in logarithmic form.

The variable definitions are found in table 4-2, and the means and standard deviations for the included variables are found in table 4-3. The equations were estimated using weighted regression techniques on the 471 observations previously described.[h] Both equations are in log-log or multiplicative form; that is, all of the variables (except the central city dummy variable) were transformed into natural logarithms before a linear regression is estimated.[i] In this case, the

[h]When aggregate relationships using average values are estimated, the use of weighted regression techniques are justified for two reasons. First, intuitively one wants to predict better where the most students are found. Second, for formal statistical reasons, if one assumes homoscedasicity for the individual student relationships, the aggregate relationship will necessarily be heteroscedastic. Therefore, for efficiency in estimation, weighted regression is used where the weights are the number of sixth grade whites.

[i]Since the natural logarithm is undefined for negative numbers and equals minus infinity for the value of zero, some care must be exercised in defining the variables before transformation.

Zero output is not a reasonable expectation if some variable is zero in the aggregate relationship. Therefore, variables which could assume zero values are redefined by adding one to them. This insures that the logarithm is greater than or equal to zero.

For interpretation, $\log Y = a + b (\log X) + c (\log Z)$ is equivalent to $Y = e^a X^b Z^c$.

Table 4-2

Variable Definitions for the White Educational Production Functions

VERBAL	mean verbal ability test score for white sixth graders
MATH	mean mathematics achievement test score for white sixth graders
CC	central city dummy variable = 1 if school is in central city of SMSA; = 0 otherwise
G	goods index; average of percentage of white sixth graders whose family owns automobile, television, refrigerator, telephone and record player
E_f	mean father's education (years) for white sixth graders
FS	mean family size (total number of people in home) for white sixth graders
NS	percentage of white sixth graders who attended nursery school
M	percentage of school population that moved away last year
HS	percentage of white sixth graders who wish to finish high school or more
S	percentage of white sixth graders who feel that people like self do not have much chance for success
T	mean teacher verbal test score (for teachers who teach in the sixth grade or lower)
E	mean years of teaching experience (for teachers who teach in the sixth grade or lower)
NT	percentage of white sixth graders who had a nonwhite teacher during the last year
N_{75-100}	Black concentration = percentage black sixth graders if greater than 75 percent; = 0 otherwise.

Table 4-3

Means and Standard Deviations for Variables in the White Educational Production Functions

Variable	Mean	Standard Deviation
VERBAL	35.70	4.54
MATH	15.85	2.15
CC	.51	
G	92.49	7.29
E_f	11.67	1.87
FS	4.48	.52
NS	15.23	14.25
M	7.79	6.88
HS	94.33	6.87
S	9.81	6.71
T	24.77	1.43
E	11.88	4.56
NT	13.42	16.03

parameters may be interpreted as elasticities.[j] In other words, a coefficient estimate of .1 indicates that a 10 percent increase in the given independent variable ceteris paribus, will result in a 1 percent increase in the dependent variable (educational achievement).[k]

The logarithmic form of the equation was chosen over the linear additive form. This form is generally more consistent with a priori views about the educational process since it both allows for interactions among variables and can exhibit diminishing marginal products. Additionally, the statistical properties of the equation seemed better; in particular, the parameter estimates were more precise (higher values of t-statistics). Given these considerations and the conceptual superiority of the logarithmic form, the logarithmic models were chosen as the better representation of the educational production process.

The most notable overall feature is that the production relationships for verbal and math are very similar. While there were conceptual reasons for expecting differences in the two equations, it is difficult to separate the two empirically. The simple correlation between math achievement and verbal ability test scores at the individual level is .70;[l] for school mean scores, this correlation is .89. The implication of this correlation is that there is very little independent variation in the two output measures.

For policy purposes it would be desirable to ascertain the reason for this high intercorrelation in test measures. There are three plausible explanations for this occurrence. First, there could be just one dimension (or slightly more) of learning in nature. This explanation implies that differences in measured output are just random noise and that no meaning should be attached to differences in parameter estimates. However, there is considerable evidence suggesting this is not the case.[7] Second, the math test might rely heavily on verbal skills so that the high correlation is merely a testing aberration. Finally, all learning in our schools (as presently organized) could be dependent upon verbal skills to a considerable extent. The last two explanations have different implications for interpreting the estimated production functions and for public policy.

If the testing reason holds, the meaning which should be attached to the MATH equation is ambiguous; it is difficult to ascertain whether it is anything different from another VERBAL production function. On the other hand, the school structure theory implies that, if different educational outputs are valued

---

[j]Note that these will be elasticities in terms of the transformed variables, i.e., after adding one to the original variables.

[k]Some care must be exercised in interpreting the parameters, as many of the variables are defined as percentages. The elasticity applies to the absolute size of the variable. Thus, a change of a variable value from 5 percent to 10 percent is a 100 percent increase in the variable.

[l]This is the simple correlation for the 26,093 individual white sixth graders in the "North" region in which the schools are found. Students were included in this calculation even though the school they attended might not be in the sample of 471. Exclusion from the regression sample arose from either missing principal data or having less than five whites in the school.

independently, major efforts should be made at either freeing parts of the curriculum or intensifying the study of basic verbal sections even at the slighting of other subjects. Unfortunately, it is impossible with these data to distinguish between the last two hypotheses. The similarity of the two equations does free us from attaching much meaning to differences in the processes, and the discussion of the estimates will explicitly consider the VERBAL estimates with only passing reference to any differences in the two equations.

The production functions are best considered in blocks which correspond roughly to the vectors of inputs in the conceptual model (Eq. 2.1). In actual practice, however, variables do not fit neatly into these vectors. While we know that the actual educational production process is very complex, the models of the process presented in Eqs. 4.1 and 4.2 necessarily simplify parts of the process and combine groups of factors together. Thus, some of the conceptual clarity is lost. Nevertheless, the crude division into these terms provides a useful taxonomy, since the policy implications differ in a systematic manner associated with the vectors.

Central Cities

The first variable in the equation (CC) is a dummy variable for central cities. If a particular school is located in the central city of an SMSA, this variable has a value of one; if it is in the suburban ring, it has a value of zero. The negative coefficient indicates that, all other inputs being equal, the expected achievement in central cities will be less than in the suburbs. The use of the dummy variable is forced by a lack of data and a certain amount of ignorance about community factors entering the production function. Certainly this variable acts as a surrogate for other conditions. The most probable factors are differences in housing conditions, the existence of ghettoes, bureaucratic rigidities (both inside and outside of the school system), fiscal pressures, attitudes toward schooling, and dynamic characteristics which differ between central city and suburb. The adjustment in the intercept of the equation is an approximation for a more complex relationship which surely exists, but for policy purposes it would be desirable to model the causes of this decrement in achievement.

The existence of this negative adjustment to the process indicates that central city students, when compared with suburban students, leave schools disadvantaged. The model implies that, with identical inputs into the process, a student in a central city school system only reaches 97.6 percent of the achievement level of the suburban school.[m] This is over and above the fact that central city students are often disadvantaged in terms of both school and nonschool inputs, which are measured by the other variables in the equation. The across-the-board

---

[m] The value of $e^{-.023}$ is .976, which is multiplied times the entire equation in calculating the predicted achievement level.

disadvantage for central city students adds an additional consideration to analysis of the distribution of educational services.

Family Background

Numerous studies have shown a positive influence of higher social and economic position on achievement.[8] Obviously, family background must be included in any properly specified model. Nevertheless, this is not an essential policy section of the educational model which we are constructing. Proper statistical analysis required adequate representation of family background; however, including this does not imply equal interest from a policy point of view. Including explicit family background measures in the models is functionally equivalent to the stratification by family occupation in chapter 3. Even if one believed that there was a causal relationship running from family background (as measured by income-related variables) to achievement, the idea of changing all income levels to bring about achievement changes is unreasonable a priori. It would be extremely expensive to alter education in this manner. Moreover, the sensible hypothesis about family background is not that one buys achievement with higher income, but that income levels do a good job of proxying a set of family characteristics which are important to education.[n] In other words, a causal relationship does not exist between income level and achievement, but between achievement and a group of other factors which are correlated with, but not necessarily causally related to, income.[o] These factors include providing a good model of language usage, encouragement in language and problem-solving development, interest in education, parental attention, and help with homework.

Social class would also be expected to enter in conjunction with innate abilities. Most people accept that genetic endowments or innate abilities have a complex effect on achievement through both an independent effect and an interaction with environment. If innate ability is partially hereditary and social mobility through ability exists, socioeconomic variables will partially proxy the

---

[n]This must be qualified at least at the lower extreme of the distribution. There are two relevant considerations at the lower end. The partial equilibrium nature of this study is crucial, since income redistributions are generally the product of other considerations and, thus, would not be evaluated solely in terms of educational benefits. Second, at the extreme it might be possible to buy education, i.e., a causal model might be applicable. To the extent that a poor diet yields permanent mental damage or even that overcrowded housing prohibits studying by an otherwise well-motivated child, achievement can be bought. Nevertheless, for the vast majority of children, the other factors proxied by contemporaneous socioeconomic status seem much more important.

[o]An additional qualifier is needed at this point. People do buy education to the extent that schools enter their residential location decision. However, this is something different from what is discussed above. People do not generally buy the family background inputs to the process. To the extent that school inputs are adequately measured, this element of "buying" education through location decision is accounted for.

unmeasured innate abilities. Further, socioeconomic variables will pick up some of the interaction effects. Thus, measured background will have an inflated effect on achievement due to model misspecification (the lack of data on innate abilities).[p] Misspecification problems are more serious here than in chapter 3 where initial achievement levels were included in the models.

The essential point in the subsequent discussion is ascertaining whether or not the measures of family inputs adequately indicate the educational differences among families. The issue is not the estimates of the coefficients for the background measures; neither is it the "importance" of background factors relative to other factors. Instead, it is the adequacy of the measures so that the accuracy of the estimates for school inputs and other policy factors can be ascertained. If family backgrounds are not adequately captured, the estimated school coefficients may well be biased, contaminated by the poorly measured factors.

The model contains three "pure" socioeconomic measures; two of these picture the income and wealth of the family while the third measures family size. (There is another set of variables which has some of the attributes of socioeconomic measures but also contains distinctive dimensions which call for division from the "pure" measures.) The goods index (G) which summarizes major items in the home and mean father's education (E_f) are the basic measures of socioeconomic status (SES). The goods index is probably the most reliable of the various possibilities for measuring SES. It is easy for a sixth grader to list major items in the home; it is not so easy to give parents' education accurately.[q] Nevertheless, family educational level, albeit less reliable, suggests a different dimension of SES, and (as compared with educational level) items in the home does not possess the same amount of intuitive meaning. It is not necessary to dwell on problems of interpretation or errors, since the parameter estimates in this section are not the most interesting for policy application. And, the choice of SES measures is not critical, since the parameter estimates in other parts of the model proved to be very stable under alternative socioeconomic measures.

Many authors have hypothesized that mother's educational level is much more important in training children than father's education, although this argument seems more applicable to the matriarchial societies found in disadvantaged neighborhoods. Nevertheless, the difference in effect cannot be examined

[p]The misspecification through missing data coupled with the hypothesized correlation with included variables causes some problems in the statistical estimation. To the extent that such a correlation between the error term and the explanatory variables occurs, the assumptions of the least squares estimation procedure fail, and the parameter estimates for socioeconomic variables will be biased and inconsistent. However, by deemphasizing the background section of the model, this does not appear to be a crucial point. It would only be important if the point estimates of the parameters would be put to some use.

[q]Parents' education questions are subject to considerable nonresponse, and this appears to be systematic. The education measures in this study assigned the nonrespondents the school mean value. While this probably yields an overestimate, there is no clearly preferable alternative.

empirically, for the simple correlation between mother's education and father's education is .79 at the school level. In this case, the problem of multicollinearity is severe enough to make estimation of individual parameters for mother's and father's education impossible.[r] Father's education is justified as it would provide a better picture of the income level. (This is quite analogous to the use of the white-collar/blue-collar distinction which became the sample stratification criterion in chapter 3). The basic modeling efforts included alternative specifications with mother's education and similar various terms. There was little effect on the overall characteristics of the model.

A final note on the goods index appears in order. The items (car, TV, telephone, refrigerator, and record player) seem very gross and unable to provide satisfactory differentiation. However, this is not the case. While there is some "topping out" of the index, it appears to do a good job of differentiating the middle and lower ranges of the social class scale. The index does have a fair amount of variation, with a standard deviation in the sample of 7.3 (mean = 92.5). Also, there exists outside evidence that there is variation in the population. In 1960 only 68 percent of central city residents owned automobiles, 81 percent had telephones, and 88 percent had televisions. For the suburban ring, these figures were 89, 86, and 93 percent, respectively.[9] This index is admittedly fairly crude but, averaged over a school, seems to capture many of the essential differences in socioeconomic status.

These two measures (the goods index and father's education) as expected have a strong influence on education. The estimates are statistically very significant and indicate very high elasticities. Nevertheless, while the importance of families has been emphasized since *EEO*, it is not the least bit surprising that family background exerts such a significant impact on achievement given that a very high percentage of a child's life is spent under the sole influence of his nonschool environment.

The last "pure" SES factor is family size (FS). There are several reasons why one expects a negative effect on achievement from increases in family size. The negative effect is consistent with a lessened attention hypothesis. With larger families there is less time to be spent with each child, each gets less help, etc. It

---

[r]When the explanatory variables are very highly correlated with each other, the independent effects of each cannot be separated. At the extreme, when a perfect linear relationship exists among the explanatory variables, it is impossible to obtain individual parameter estimates. The more usual case is that the variables approach a linear dependency. With this it is not possible to obtain parameter estimates with any precision. Some feel for the extent of collinearity between father's and mother's education can be derived from the value of the determinant of the correlation matrix. With orthogonal variables this has a value of one; with linear dependent variables it has a value of zero. As suggested by Farrar and Glauber in the "The Problem of Multicollinearity Revisited," *Review of Economics and Statistics*, February 1967, the range between the extremes has not been mapped out. However, on the step at which both variables are entered the determinant goes from .12 to .0004, a dramatic enough change to indicate the inseparability of effects of the two variables.

is also consistent with a standard of living adjustment, i.e., that wealth (goods index) must be adjusted for family size to consider different costs. This is very plausible in the multiplicative formulation of the model. However, it is not possible to hold strictly to this interpretation as a standard of living adjustment must consider family makeup, e.g., whether two adults are present. Also, the marginal costs of additional children are probably not truly measured by our constant elasticity model (and even less so in a linear model which includes something like per capita wealth). Nevertheless, this overall adjustment appears reasonably good with a t-statistic of 2.3, and, for our purposes, it is unnecessary to sort out the alternative hypotheses which could account for a negative relationship.

The *OE Survey* does contain other measures, both objective and subjective, of family background. Most notable is the occupation variable included in the student questionnaires. However, the combination of poor formulation and nonresponse or faulty response led to the exclusion of this measure.[10] Other objective measures such as structural integrity of the home were evaluated, but judged insignificant. Several subjective measures were also tested, but found to be statistically insignificant. (These measures will be discussed in more detail later.)

The three measures of socioeconomic status used in the model appear to capture most of the important dimensions of environment in the learning process. While they strictly apply to only contemporaneous factors, there do not appear to be large errors in variables, at least at the school level. Since these factors are all so highly intercorrelated, little is gained by adding more SES variables. These factors exhibit a very stable effect on achievement, independent of specific formulations of the remaining effects on achievement, that is independent of the measurement of school effects on achievement.

Pre-School

Nursery school (NS) represents a combination of factors. Partly it measures another dimension of socioeconomic position; it offers vivid proof of parents' interest in the education of their children. Additionally, and more importantly for policy purposes, it appears to measure the effect of earlier training. To the extent that the latter holds, there is confirmation of an often hypothesized, crucial effect of starting early in the learning process. This early impact derives from the sequential nature of learning and the rapid development before age six.[11] There is no strong test for separating these two factors with the data from the *OE Survey*. However, indirect tests indicate that the early schooling hypothesis could well be the stronger. Various measures of parental attitudes and interest in education were modeled, but none showed a significant influence on achievement, even when nursery school was excluded from the model.[S] This indicates that we can be a little more confident in accepting the straightforward pre-school hypothesis.

While the elasticity of .004 on the surface indicates that this exerts a weak influence on achievement, there are reasons to believe that the effect could be considerably larger. This variable is subject to considerable error in measurement since all nursery schools are rated as being of equal quality. In reality there is known to be a large variance in quality and quantity of schooling among pre-schools. In quality terms, there are "organized play" programs and more scholastically orientated programs such as Headstart. In quantity terms, there are large differences in both length of day and number of days for the program. Such errors in measurement would lead to a downward bias in the estimated parameter.[12] On the other hand, direct evaluations of Headstart program find little lasting effect.[13]

The fact that any effect of nursery schooling is found in the sampled sixth graders, after seven years, is somewhat surprising. And, the indications that the effect might be larger than pictured are encouraging, since nursery school programs represent a readily available policy tool. Certainly more research into this area is needed, but even now this is becoming an increasingly popular policy suggestion.[14]

Migration

The percentage of the school population that moved away during the past year, M, has the expected negative relationship with achievement. This is consistent with two plausible hypotheses about the educational process. The most obvious interpretation is that there is a cost in terms of continuity attached with moving. This disruption factor for the individual students involved is sure to be present. Moreover, it can also affect teaching. If a school has a very high turnover, it is difficult to map a sequential learning program through the grades. When a high percentage of a class starts at different levels, the teaching must be revised from the situation where everybody starts together. This cannot help but have a detrimental effect on learning when compared to schools with low migration rates.

[S]The *OE Survey* includes several questions about parental attitudes as perceived by the student. For example, in a multiple choice framework, how good a student does your mother want you to be in school? How often do you and your parents talk about your school work? These questions were transformed into percentages for the school, e.g., percent with pushy mothers (percent whose mother wished above average performance). Certainly these are not ideal data on attitudes. However, the fact that none of them will demonstrate a significant influence on education, even when nursery school is excluded, provides some evidence that nursery school is not solely, or even chiefly, another socioeconomic variable measuring an attitude dimension.

While the elasticity estimate of .006 appears quite low, the possibility of large differences in migration rates exists. The model indicates, ceteris paribus, that doubling the migration rate is associated with a .6 percent decline in mean achievement. Within the sample, there are frequent cases of migration rates for schools within the same city differing by a factor of ten, e.g., ranging from 2 percent to 20 percent. With other factors held constant, a change from the low to the high migration rate would yield a 6 percent drop in the achievement level.

This is, in many ways, another educational handicap falling upon children of lower socioeconomic status families. Migration rates within metropolitan areas are consistently higher for lower income families.

The relationship of migration and achievement do not lead immediately to policy, at least without other information. Policies to reduce migration tend to be unappealing. On the other hand, there are no simple solutions to how the impact of migration can be handled.

Attitudes

The attitudes of the student are another set of variables which are related to socioeconomic background. The chief reason for splitting these away from the socioeconomic variables is that these measures relate directly to the individual as opposed to his family. As such they are under the control of the individual, and, even though they might be influenced by family socioeconomic factors, these subjective factors are clearly produced by a complex process which includes more than just family SES.

Two principle attitude measures were used in the production functions which were estimated. The first, reflecting the educational aspirations of the student body, is the percentage of students who wish to complete high school or more (HS). As expected, high educational desires are associated with high achievement. This displays a very significant effect ($t = 4.4$), and the elasticity is quite high, .29 in VERBAL production and .42 in MATH production.

The other attitude variable (S) measures fate control. Higher values of S are associated with greater pessimism as more students think that "people like me don't have much of a chance to be successful in life." As one would expect, this negative attitude exhibits a detrimental effect on achievement. However, the low elasticity of .03 indicates that it does not have an overpowering influence on achievement.

The interpretation of attitudes is not as simple, however, as suggested above. First, for many reasons it would be desirable to know how attitudes are formed. Attitudes are not changed by decree. People often attempt to promote more healthy attitudes as in television commercials advocating staying in school or suggesting the wide range of vocational opportunities available. If these methods will affect attitudes, the production functions suggest that they will have favorable effects on the quality of education. Attitude formation is also of interest when considering the effects of schools on achievement. For policy purposes we would like to know the total effect of school factors on education. Therefore, if school inputs (teachers, facilities, and curriculum) have an effect on attitudes, the direct effect given by the estimated parameters for school inputs will understate their total effect on achievement. While we are unable to specify and estimate a complete attitude formation model, we can gain some insight into the extent of this indirect effect on achievement of school inputs. By eliminating the attitude variables from the equation, we obtain an upper bound on the indirect effect through attitudes. When this is done, there is practically no effect on the school inputs.[15]

A more serious consideration in interpreting the results is the possibility that attitudes and achievement are simultaneously determined. This is the case if the student includes indications of his achievement in forming attitudes. When this is the case, the statistical assumptions underlying the least squares estimation procedure fail, the parameter estimates are biased and inconsistent,[16] and least squares is not the appropriate estimation technique.

However, two factors enter into deciding upon this point. First, even though specification of the attitude model is a hazardous task in itself, the roughest a priori specification of this model would include many essential factors for which we have no data, e.g., neighborhood and housing characteristics, attitudes of friends and siblings, etc. Most substitutes for least squares regression techniques require specification of the system of equations and data for the specified exogeneous variables in the system. Secondly, there are a priori reasons to believe that the simultaneity might not be "too great" in the sixth grade. The simultaneity arises when the student readjusts his goals due to cues from achievement. However, one could imagine that there have not been enough cues or strong enough cues for the majority of the students to need much revision in aspirations and attitudes formed elsewhere. If the simultaneity is not large, that is achievement is not one of the prime determinants of attitudes, the parameter estimates from ordinary least squares techniques will approach consistent estimates, and one might opt for this more efficient procedure.[17] This is the route followed here, especially since the missing attitude formation factors would result in very inefficient estimates if instrumental variable techniques were used with the given data.

Again the major policy implications are found elsewhere in the model. Attitudes were included in order to achieve better overall model specification. The lack of a good attitude formation model severely limits any policy aimed at altering attitudes so as to increase educational output. Additionally, the uncertainty about the properties of the parameter estimates causes hesitancy in placing great weight on this section of the model.

School Effects

The remainder of the model holds more interest for us. This section describes the effects of schools on achievement. Since the publication of *Equality of Educational Opportunity*, it has been widely circulated that schools have no effect on achievement. There are a number of conceptual and methodological reasons why one should expect this result. These issues are discussed at length elsewhere.[18] However, these articles merely suggest why *EEO* fails to provide a reasonable test of the effect of schools on achievement; they do not show that the real situation is one where there is a significant school effect on achievement. Chapter 3 offers direct evidence about the effects of school. The models of education presented in Eqs. 4.1 and 4.2 also offer evidence that the *EEO* view is not an accurate portrayal of education in the United States. Schools do have a significant effect on achievement. The models presented here for whites (and in chapter 5 for blacks) demonstrate that even the crude measures of school factors which we have appear significant in describing the educational production process. The popular interpretations of *EEO* could only leave one extremely pessimistic about the educational system. Yet these results suggest that much of the pessimism may be unwarranted.

There are three school input measures included in this analysis. These are the average score on the teacher verbal test *(T)*, the average years of teacher experience *(E)*, and the percentage of students who had a nonwhite teacher during the past year *(NT)*. Taken together, these indicate a considerable effect from schools and, in particular, higher quality teachers.

The teacher verbal test score represents the best measure of teacher quality contained in the data. This provides a method of making standardized comparisons across teachers. Nevertheless, this is a crude measure of teacher quality at best. This gives some measure of technical competence of the teaching staff in one particular dimension—verbal ability.[t] However, there are many other dimensions of teaching which cannot be measured by this. For example, rapport with the class, empathy, warmth, cogent presentations, and knowledge of subject matter are all valuable facets of teaching. The verbal test measure of quality touches on none of these factors.

Given these shortcomings, the magnitude of the effect is significant. The elasticity of .13 for such a poorly measured indicator of teacher quality provides considerable encouragement in the ability of schools to affect children.[19] The

---

[t]It has been suggested that this might also measure the collective technical ability of the faculty due to collusion in the taking of the test. However, this is merely speculation. Additionally, even if this were the case, it is not obvious that it is that harmful when school means are used. There might be some upward bias in each score, but for our purposes the variation among schools is more important, i.e., whether schools still fall in the same relative position.

reduced elasticity (.09) and greater imprecision of the estimate ($t = 1.3$) in the math production function lends support to a strict technical capabilities interpretation of the test score variable as opposed to a broader, overall ability interpretation. This provides another piece of evidence that the test is quite incomplete and suggests that better measures of "teaching ability" would show a stronger relationship with achievement. The elasticity estimate is also less than the school elasticities found in chapter 3 where there was better measurement.

Table 4-3 indicates that there is a small amount of variation in this measure with a standard deviation of only 1.4 and a mean of 24.8 (maximum possible score equals 30). Nevertheless, redistributions of teachers, even within the same city, can have a significant impact on mean school achievement. For example, within one sampled city there exist differences of 40 percent in mean teacher verbal test scores. If these faculties were switched, the mean achievement level in the lower quality school would increase by 4.5 percent. (The experience levels of these faculties were roughly equal.) Additionally there are a number of reasons, which will be mentioned later, to believe that this significantly underestimates the actual increase that would occur if such a change were undertaken.

Teacher experience also exhibits a significant effect on achievement. The presence of more experienced teachers is positively correlated with achievement. Thus, over and above other quality factors, teaching experience helps. Certainly one would expect a positive effect of experience in comparing the first year or two of teaching with subsequent years. However, this indicates that it holds true for the whole spectrum of teaching experience.[u] Again, while the effect does not appear overpowering with an elasticity of .02, a significant relationship with achievement is indicated. This is an interesting contrast to the findings in chapter 3.

With the experience measure some care must be exercised in interpretation, however. Given the prevalence of "seniority rights" in city school systems which allow the more senior teachers to choose their school, part of the experience influence is undoubtedly due to a school selection phenomenon. However, indirect evidence arising from the insignificance of explicit measures of selection implies that there exists a pure experience effect.[20]

The final measure of teacher quality is the percentage of sixth graders who had a nonwhite teacher during the last year. This is interpreted as a measure of part of the teacher quality distribution, i.e., the lower end of the teacher distribution. This interpretation arises from our knowledge of the education provided to blacks. Many studies, including a survey of colleges presented in *EEO* show the general quality gap between blacks and whites who go into teaching.[21] This is not particularly surprising given that blacks are given inferior

---

[u]Note that this is not a linear effect, however. There is a nonlinear relationship implied by the logarithmic transformation of the variables. Other nonlinear forms were tested by dividing experience into ranges (e.g., 1-5 years, 5-10 years, etc.). No significant differences were found there.

elementary and secondary school education and then proceed to segregated colleges which tend to widen the educational gap (by race). Thus, the nonwhite teacher variable tends to capture the lower end of the distribution of teachers.

It is interesting that NT has such a small standard error connected with the parameter estimate ($t = 6.8$). This variable is the most accurately measured school factor that is found in the data for this applies to the particular students in question and does relate specific students to specific inputs.[v] By doing this, a priori one would expect less error in this particular variable and indeed the precision of the estimate indicates that this is true.

It is particularly apropos when assessing the importance of the school variables to consider the errors present in the variables. The conceptual model presented in Eq. 2.1 suggested that the whole past history of school inputs relevant to the particular individual were important in modeling the educational process. When we went from the individual model to the school model, we did not eliminate the requirement for having the past history of school factors nor for having those pertaining to the individuals in the aggregate production function. We fall far short of having this information. The essential problems revolve around migration—both teacher and student. To the extent that any migration occurs, errors are introduced into our school measures. When this is considered in the standard errors in variables format, it can be shown that the coefficients will necessarily be biased downward.[22] While it is not possible to know the extent of any bias, it is known that an average of 45 percent of the sixth graders in the sample have attended at least one other school and an average of 8.8 percent of the teachers in each school left during the past year. These figures only provide some idea of the potential bias. Without further knowledge about the educational production function, it is impossible to assess the magnitude of bias. For example, if the process attaches declining weights to more distant experiences, the migration figures tend to overstate the size of potential bias. However, it is plausible that the early experiences count *more* in the process.[23] If this is the case, the errors as indicated in the migration figures could be quite substantial.

The study of school production functions does confound the issue of errors in variables in the teacher inputs. Certainly there is a potential for error by considering teachers which none of the sixth graders under study have had, e.g., new teachers to the school in the lower grades. However, the school figures for teacher ability and experience are not necessarily bad measures of school inputs for the students under consideration. The important consideration is the dynamic allocation process by which teachers are hired by the school. To the extent that "school character" is stable over time, the school averages of contemporaneous faculty could provide fair pictures of the historical inputs to the students.

---

[v]This variable comes from the student questionnaire and, thus, relates to the specific teacher which the student had in the past year as opposed to the school-wide average.

In summary, the estimated model of the educational process is quite encouraging. Even though the measures of school quality are crude and error prone, a strong relationship between our measures and achievement is found to exist. The measurement problems also suggest that our estimates are, in fact, minimum estimates of the effects of schools on achievement. There are a number of reasons to expect that the actual point estimates of the educational parameters are biased toward zero. Thus, if one starts with the impression given by the *EEO* that schools don't matter, these results, coupled with chapter 3, provide some reason for optimism.

The *OE Survey* does contain additional measures of teacher quality, and several other aspects of the teachers were included in the models, but proved insignificant in their effect on achievement. These included the percentage of teachers with a master's degree or more, percentage male teachers,[24] percentage of teachers who read educational journals, choice of schools, percentage without teaching certificate,[w] percentage who are leaving teaching after present school year, and average age of teaching staff. Certainly there are many measurement problems with these variables, and caution must be exercised in inferring that these have no effect on achievement. The errors in measurement will affect the significance levels. Nonetheless, within this sample and the data limitations, the various dimensions of teacher quality represented by these specific variables prove to have no effect.

One specific hypothesis should be mentioned. A commonly used measure of school inputs is per student expenditure.[25] While there is no measure of total per pupil expenditures for each school,[26] it is possible to construct a measure of instructional expenditures per pupil for each school from the teacher salary data. Since instructional expenditures comprise about 70 percent of current operating expenditures, this seems to be a worthwhile test of the usefulness of per pupil expenditures as a measure of the provision of school inputs.

This variable has an insignificant effect on achievement in the model of the educational process. This holds even if other measures of school inputs are excluded from the relationship. However, by itself this should not be entirely interpreted that school systems are operating inefficiently. While per pupil expenditures would not be a good measure of school quality if schools did act inefficiently, i.e., did not spend their budgets on inputs so as to maximize output, there are other plausible explanations of finding no relationship between expenditures and output. If school inputs did not matter in the educational production process, there would be no significant relationship. However, the other evidence in the models presented suggests this is not the case. There is

---

[w]Obviously this variable is quite weak in this cross-state study where there are very different requirements for certification. Also, there are complexities introduced since those without certificates might be higher quality as lack of certification could indicate majoring in something other than education and not going to a teachers college. This is further confused by the fact that many without certificates are actually substitute teachers. High levels of substitutes would be expected to have a negative effect on achievement.

another, and very plausible, explanation for this phenomenon. In the presence of sizable differences in factor prices, comparisons of per student expenditures lose their meaning. It is believed that this is the situation in the sample for the region is quite large and inhomogeneous in terms of input price. Large price variations are known to exist even within metropolitan areas.[27] Thus, without the aid of a price index, one cannot expect per pupil expenditures to act as a good index of school quality. The single system analysis in chapter 3 did provide, nevertheless, strong evidence for the inefficiency hypothesis.

Black Concentration

The preliminary modeling efforts involved the percentage black as a continuous variable. The obvious hypothesis tested was that either classroom disruption due to racial tension or differences of black backgrounds (with an adjustment in teaching techniques) led to a reduction in the education of whites. However, the independent effect of racial composition on whites was insignificant when measured in this manner. A second hypothesis tested was that there is a differential effect for different degrees of racial mixing, along with the possibility of threshold effects of racial composition. In order to test this, the percentage black sixth graders was divided into a number of mutually exclusive ranges. For example, there was one variable equal to the percentage black if less than 25 percent and equal to zero otherwise; there was another for the range 25 percent to 45 percent; etc.

For white achievement the only significant range for racial composition was 75 to 100 percent black (N_{75-100}).[x] (The parameter estimates for all other ranges were less than their standard errors.) Additionally, this factor is only important in the VERBAL production process. The construct of this variable leads to some interpretative problems since a literal acceptance of this formulation implies that white achievement falls by 13 percent when the racial mix goes from 74 to 75 percent black. It is doubtful that a precise threshold exists, and the paucity of schools within this upper range makes the cut-off arbitrary. A better interpretation of this variable is that racial composition does not affect white achievement until the school is two-thirds to three-quarters black. After such a point, there is a steady decline in white achievement. (There is no significant intercept difference when these continuous concentration variables are used in the model.)

The explanation of this decline appears to be imbedded more in poor measurement of the various factors than in racial tensions. There are several factors which could contribute to this negative relationship. The most plausible

[x]There are nine schools in the white sample which fall in this range of racial composition. While this number is small, it is encouraging that only two are in the same SMSA, and, thus, this variable is not just measuring one poor school system.

explanation is that these are especially poor schools and that the measures of school quality do not adequately distinguish these extreme schools. Furthermore, measurement of socioeconomic factors must be considered as these whites are people who, although not faced with housing discrimination, are living in the ghetto. It could well be that the measures of SES used in the analysis are unable to distinguish the tail of the distribution, and this is a measure of whites who cannot because of poverty, ignorance, or whatever move from the black ghetto.

Facilities

Throughout the discussion of school effects the real issue was teacher effects on achievement. To the economist this seems to be the natural place to look for school effects as instructional expenditures represent 70 percent of variable costs and 55 percent of total costs.[28] Thus, any presumption of rationality in resource allocation indicates that indeed teachers are what count. Nevertheless, it appears that sociologists and educators do not look at the problem in this manner. *EEO* in particular often tends to speak only of facilities and curriculum when analyzing school inputs and their effects.[29] First it is apparent that this leads to confusion in assessing the *EEO* findings. However, past the semantics of the issue, there is a more substantive point. Conceptually, it is far from obvious that facilities are going to have a strong direct effect on achievement. A seemingly better model of education pictures tinted windows, green boards, and the like as entering into attitude formation and, thus, only indirectly into achievement.[y] Even here, the expected effect on attitudes is not strong. At least this is the case for any causal element which is what is important for policy purposes. It could well be that parents with strong interest in education will support more elaborate and better maintained facilities. In such an instance it is hard to claim that the facilities motivate (cause) good attitudes in the students.

Nevertheless, even if others do not support these a priori views, the *OE Survey* does not provide the data required to test many hypotheses about facilities effects. Probably the weakest aspect of the survey is the measurements of the school plant and curriculum. The survey is riddled with nonresponse to specific questions. Since there is only one source of this data (the principal), errors cannot be reduced by averaging as in the case of student data.

Furthermore the questions are very insensitive to quality differences and neglect many important aspects of the school. For example, a biology laboratory can be defined by a cabinet housing a microscope and possibly a nearby washbasin. Merely asking the principal whether the school has a biology laboratory or not does not gain much information (especially given natural pride which would tend to lead to liberal definitions by principals).

[y]This would be modified at the extreme where physical discomfort, noise, or overcrowding may limit teacher effectiveness.

The lack of qualitative features is particularly noticeable, and such low information questions are prevalent in more than descriptions of the physical plant. There are numerous examples of weak or omitted questions about school structure. There is little information on the school organization, e.g., the use of specialized teachers. And, while there are a few questions about the use ability grouping or tracking, they are so broad and open to such diverse interpretation that they do not appear to be reliable measures. In terms of facilities and organization, it is even difficult to model such apparently straightforward aspects as class sizes and numbers per room. This arises from the considerable error in coding these variables and a range of conceptual difficulties. Further there are obvious conceptual difficulties; overall pupil-teacher ratios for a school do not provide a very good analog to the conceptual input of effective class sizes. Schools may choose to have larger classes, but more specialized teachers and more free time for teachers; the differences in length of school days in itself provides a difficult problem in analyzing the effects of class sizes on the educational process. This modeling problem is not atypical of those found in the facilities and curriculum section of the model.

Measuring facility inputs for the sample of schools is further complicated by the heterogeneity of organization. Some schools are first through sixth; some first through eighth; some fourth through eighth. The particular organization has a definite effect on facilities, e.g., presence of science labs, libraries, etc. However, when these facilities are provided for eighth graders, it is not necessarily true that they are relevant to sixth graders. Information for teachers can be restricted to cover only those teaching sixth grade or below; facilities cannot be easily segregated in this manner.

Numerous additional examples of data problems can easily be found. However, the above examples appear sufficient to establish the case of the crudeness of facilities and curriculum measures. Thus, even though several measures of school facilities and characteristics were attempted (but discarded) in modeling the educational production process, it is difficult to consider such efforts a legitimate test of the effects of plant and curriculum on achievement.[z] Even if one does not a priori wish to discount the importance of facility items in the educational process, the data are insufficient to construct reasonable tests of the various facilities hypotheses which are made.

---

[z]Among the measures of school inputs other than teachers attempted were percentage students attending less than normal day, library volumes per student, presence of special classes for rapid learners and adjustment problems, average attendance rate, presence of remedial reading and math classes, number of remedial reading teachers per student, guidance counselors per student, use of high and low tracking, overall pupil-teacher ratio, presence of a librarian, and age of main buildings. There are numerous problems with each of these variables, not the least of which is nonresponse of varying degrees. Most variables were heavily edited to eliminate obvious errors and to fill in values for nonresponses.

The Education of Whites

The picture of the educational process presented in Eqs. 4.1 and 4.2 is a highly simplified view of a complex relationship. Yet, while the crude measures of inputs and the aggregative nature of the variables confuse some interpretations, the overall lesson is quite clear. Contrary to the popular interpretation of *EEO* findings, white achievement is significantly affected by the schools and, in particular, by teacher quality.

The collection of teacher inputs considered in the models have a significant effect upon the output of the schools. Additionally, there are a number of reasons to believe that the parameter estimates for these teacher measures are biased toward zero. While it is not possible to ascertain the extent of this bias, the potential size of errors of this kind is great. This implies that teacher quality has a greater effect on achievement than a literal interpretation of the production function would indicate. The small parameter estimate for experience and the insignificance of graduate education does, however, provide support of the previous, single-system findings of inefficiencies in the public schools. This would indicate that schools are generally purchasing the wrong set of characteristics.

5 Multisystem Analysis — Black Education

It is time to start dealing with the hard, cruel facts of the problem of the ghetto schools, which is in turn the very core of the race problem in the United States.[1]

While the web of racial discrimination and racial conflict is complex, there is little question that black education is central to the problem. It remains to be answered, however, how one should approach the objective set forth above by Joseph Alsop of dealing with the ghetto schools. This chapter lends insight into the "how" through the presentation of empirical evidence on the educational production process for blacks, while chapter 6 considers interracial aspects of public education, namely de facto segregation and racial composition of the school.

The analysis of educational production functions for black sixth graders is perfectly analogous to the modeling efforts for whites presented in the previous chapter. Within the same conceptual framework and using the same data source, school production functions for blacks were estimated. The study of the educational process was divided into separate studies of the education of whites and the education of blacks for two reasons. First, the extent of psychological, economic, and cultural differences between blacks and whites led to the a priori belief that the structure of the educational process might well differ between the two. If, as reasonably expected, there are different behavioral relationships in the two cases, the stratification of the school population is a necessary precondition for estimation of the production function. Second, and somewhat subtler, is the notion that the economic and cultural differences between the black and the white population imply an inconsistency in the measurement of many socioeconomic factors when blacks and whites are considered together. As explained in the discussion of the white production function section, several variables are used to measure current socioeconomic status, but their importance is more in terms of the implied parental attitudes and home environment than in terms of current income and wealth. These measures simply act as good surrogates for a collection of factors directly related to educational achievement. However, the same nominal variables measuring SES may not have equivalent meanings when taken across racial lines. It is easy to see that such measurement considerations could also enter into student attitude variables. The simple point of this discussion is that the variable definitions possibly do not represent the same unit of measurement for blacks and whites. If there is a different relationship between these income-related factors and the home educational environment in the white and the black community, it is inappropriate to consider whites and blacks together in the production process. These are identical to the reasons for stratifying the single system analysis that was presented in chapter 3.

The estimated production functions for black sixth graders are qualitatively very similar to those for white sixth graders. The overall model specifications are practically identical. More than that, the policy implications are extremely similar. Schools, as measured by the teaching staff, do have a significant effect on the achievement of blacks. Again, while there are reasons to suspect that the estimated parameters understate the actual relationships which exist, the estimates do provide encouragement as to the strength of schools in determining achievement.

Black Sample

The black sample is made up of 242 schools in the metropolitan North which have over four black sixth graders.[a] In the process of going to large schools (over four blacks) 141 sampled schools with one to four blacks were discarded. A majority of the discarded schools fell within the suburban ring, and the percentage of schools in the central city went from 62 percent to 76 percent when the sample was reduced. Nevertheless, the data problems seem sufficiently large to justify this exclusion of schools.

The mean percentage black in the sixth grade is 50 percent. However, this belies the true character of the distribution of schools as the distribution tends to be bimodal. The entire distribution is depicted in Table 5-1. The nature of the distribution of schools is not surprising from what we know about the extent of housing market segregation in metropolitan areas.[2]

Table 5-1
Distribution of Black Schools by Percentage of Sixth Graders Who Are Black

	Percentage Black										
	None	0-10	10-20	20-30	30-40	40-50	50-60	60-70	70-80	80-90	90-100
No. of Schools	0	22	39	24	30	12	21	17	21	35	21
Percentage	0	9	16	10	12	5	9	7	9	14	9

[a]The included states with the number of sample schools are: Connecticut (11), Delaware (3), Illinois (5), Indiana (9), Maine (0), Maryland (10), Massachusetts (1), Michigan (33), New Hampshire (0), New Jersey (23), New York (52), Ohio (9), Pennsylvania (49), Rhode Island (0), Vermont (0), Washington, D.C. (11), and Wisconsin (26).

Educational Production Functions for Black
Sixth Graders

The estimates of the educational production functions for blacks were quite satisfactory. They exhibited statistically strong relationships which were consistent with a priori views about the process. Eqs. 5.1 and 5.2 represent models estimated by weighted regression techniques from the 242 observations of black schools. Variable definitions are found in table 5-2, and sample means and standard deviations are displayed in table 5-3. Again, the log-log specification was judged superior to the simple linear functional form. Both conceptual reasons and statistical findings suggested this multiplicative form.

The overall model of the process is qualitatively very similar to that for white education.

$$
\begin{aligned}
\text{VERBAL*} \quad = \quad &-2.47 \; - \; .040CC \; + \; .666G* \; + \; .035E_f^* \; - \; .170FS* \\
&(-4.2) \quad\; (-2.4) \qquad (7.9) \qquad\;\; (1.2) \qquad\;\; (-2.8) \\[4pt]
&+ \; .578HS* \; - \; .027S* \; + \; .164T* \; + \; .045E* \; - \; .024NT* \\
&\quad (5.4) \qquad\quad (-2.2) \qquad (1.9) \qquad\;\; (2.6) \qquad\;\; (-1.7) \\[4pt]
&- .012N_{45-75}^* \; - \; .007N_{75-100}^* \\
&\quad (-2.9) \qquad\qquad\;\; (-1.7)
\end{aligned}
$$

$$R^2 = .58 \qquad\qquad SE = .56 \qquad\qquad (5.1)$$

$$
\begin{aligned}
\text{MATH*} \quad = \quad &-1.58 \; + \; .429G* \; + \; .061E_f^* \; - \; .193FS* \\
&(-2.4) \qquad (4.7) \qquad\;\; (1.5) \qquad\;\; (-2.9) \\[4pt]
&+ .497HS* \; - \; .036S* \; + \; .085E* \; - \; .021NT* \\
&\quad (4.0) \qquad\;\; (-2.6) \qquad (4.3) \qquad\;\; (-1.3) \\[4pt]
&- \; .017N_{45-75}^* \; - \; .012N_{75-100}^* \\
&\quad (-3.4) \qquad\qquad\;\; (-3.0)
\end{aligned}
$$

$$SE = .66 \qquad\qquad (5.2)$$

---

*Asterisks denote logarithms of variables. t-statistics are displayed in parentheses below each coefficient. SE is the standard error of estimate.

The estimates of the parameters for black education are slightly less precise, and the overall model for blacks is not as good as for whites with a standard error of estimate equal to .56 (as opposed to .38 for whites).[b] Nevertheless, the models

---

[b]The figures for the standard error of estimate in the VERBAL equation result from the weighted regression analysis in the logarithmic form. Thus, there is some difficulty in attaching meaning to the absolute values. However, the comparison between models (of the same output measure) does have meaning. The output measures for blacks and whites were arrived at from the same tests and reflect positions in the same total population. The comparable figures for MATH standard errors are: black, .66; white, .49.

Table 5-2
Variable Definitions for the Black Educational Production Functions

VERBAL mean verbal ability test score for black sixth graders

MATH mean mathematics achievement test score for black sixth graders

CC central city dummy variable = 1 if school is in central city of SMSA; = 0 otherwise

G goods index; average of percentage of black sixth graders whose family owns automobile, television, refrigerator, telephone and record player

E_f mean father's education (years) for black sixth graders

FS mean family size (total number of people in home) for black sixth graders

HS percentage of black sixth graders who wish to finish high school or more

S percentage of black sixth graders who feel that people like self do not have much chance for success

T mean teacher verbal test score (for teachers who teach in the sixth grade or lower)

E mean years of teaching experience (for teachers who teach in the sixth grade or lower)

NT percentage of black sixth graders who had a nonwhite teacher during the last year

N_{75-100} Black concentration = percentage black sixth graders if greater than 75 percent; = 0 otherwise

N_{45-75} Black concentration = percentage of black sixth graders if between 45 and 75 percent; = 0 otherwise

Table 5-3
Means and Standard Deviations for Variables in the Black Educational Production Functions

Variable	Mean	Standard Deviation
VERBAL	26.68	4.20
MATH	11.05	1.78
CC	.76	
G	84.52	8.37
E_f	10.60	1.90
FS	5.08	.65
M	10.94	7.43
HS	92.14	6.67
S	18.61	9.95
T	23.98	1.80
E	11.29	4.00
NT	44.72	19.38

do very well at portraying the basic input-output relationships in the education of black sixth graders. The parameter estimates are reasonable, and the relationships are statistically very strong.

The VERBAL and MATH production processes are very similar, although there is a larger difference between the two black models than was the case in the two for whites. The simple correlation of the verbal ability and mathematics achievement test score at the individual level is .66;[c] at the school level this correlation is .81. This value suggests that there is a fairly small amount of independent variation between the measures. The differences in the models will be interpreted as if the nominal titles of the output dimension apply. However, the high correlations, similar to those encountered in the white sample, lead to some suspicion about the differences in the tests and whether they measure what they purport to measure. The possibility that the difference between the measures is simply a random error cannot be disregarded.

The great similarity of the hypotheses about the educational process for blacks and whites suggests analyzing the resultant black models by contrasting them to the white models. A cursory glance at the models indicates a considerable correspondence between the overall models. This similarity should not be interpreted as an arbitrary decision to present equivalent models of the process. On the contrary, the black and white modeling efforts were carried out in relative isolation from each other. The best models, according to the criteria of a priori acceptability and statistical reliability, proved to be very similar in overall specification. While these modeling efforts are by no means independent of each other, as they rely upon the same data source, the similarity is encouraging since it provides prima facie evidence for the existence of a consistent set of underlying behavioral patterns in terms of school inputs to the educational process.

The remaining sections of this chapter will compare the estimated production functions for blacks with those for whites. The main emphasis is on differences between the two in the underlying hypotheses about the process; in the interpretation of the models; and in the parameter estimates. While the caveats from the previous section are equally as applicable, they will not be restated in this section. Also, the various modeling efforts described in the previous section will not be explicitly reconsidered here. It seems profitable to shift the emphasis to specific aspects of the models, especially differences between the black and white educational process.

Some Minor Differences

The overall model specification differs between blacks and whites in two variables. The black production process includes neither nursery school

cThis is computed for the 10,286 individual black sixth graders in the sample region. Again, not all of these individuals will be in the 242 included schools.

influences (NS) nor migration influences (M). There is little that can be said about this difference in specification. Migration and nursery school had the smallest elasticities of any variables in the white production function. Thus, their exclusion from the black model does not indicate a major structural difference. Additionally, both variables are measured with considerable error. The error could have been sufficient to mask any real behavioral relationship which might exist (and which is suggested by their inclusion in the white model). However, this is pure speculation.

It might be noted, however, that past experiences have indicated that any immediate advantages offered by early schooling such as Headstart or nursery school can be obliterated by poor subsequent schooling experiences. This factor could enter into the black equations with more force as the probability of lower levels of school inputs for blacks is higher.[3]

A further minor difference is found in the influence of the central city. Residing in the central city has a mixed effect in the education of blacks. In VERBAL production the estimated effects of the core city (CC) is slightly greater for blacks than for whites (although this difference is not statistically significant). The VERBAL output of the central city black school, ceteris paribus, will be 96 percent that of the suburban black school. However, central city education appears to have no bearing on MATH production. The most plausible explanation for the differential impact of central cities centers upon the errors in variable problem.

The central city dummy is used as an approximation for a series of factors which systematically differ between central city and suburb. As in the white models, both a lack of knowledge and a lack of data prevented taking any steps toward specifying and estimating the underlying influences which are associated with central cities. Nevertheless, one would expect the severity of the central city and suburb differences to vary among SMSAs. If this is the case, the dummy variable specification is incorrect and will only give an average effect for the different central cities.

There are also reasons to suspect that the measurement problems would be worse for blacks than for whites. The special characteristic of housing market discrimination and the subsequent presence of black ghettoes surely enters into the educational process through the central city dummy. There are sizable differences among cities in the conditions which produce the urban black environment. There are differences in the housing stock, e.g., age and density. There are differences in the level of provision of municipal services; for example, police and fire protection, garbage collection and street cleaning, and the system of welfare payments. Additionally, the central city and suburb differences are much sharper in the case of the black, who often faces a restricted residential location choice. It is not choice that leads blacks to opt for the ghetto tenement. To the extent that there is a larger variance in relevant attributes among central cities for the black population than for the white population *and* to the extent that the central city and suburb division is sharper and more meaningful, the poor specification from the use of the dummy variable weighs more heavily on the black model. Another set of errors is also present. In some cases, for example in the industrial suburb, the classification of a school as suburban may be simply nominal. In considering the two samples of schools, this type of error will be more severe for blacks than for whites. The errors in variables introduced by this specification will tend to bias the coefficient toward zero. The possibility of fairly severe errors in this area could go a long way toward explaining why the central city appears to enter in VERBAL production and not in MATH, and the possibility of differing importance of the errors also makes black-white comparisons tenuous. We can only conclude that the proper specification of the real factors entering into the central city differences would be useful, especially since many of these are amenable to public policy.

Family Background and Attitudes

Direct comparisons of the individual components of family background do not appear profitable. Since the model of the educational process relies upon income and wealth measures as proxies for a much larger and more complex set of attitudes, interests, and educational backgrounds, comparisons of parameter estimates are meaningful only if the transformation between income and the relevant background attributes is the same for blacks and whites. There are good a priori reasons to believe that the transformation is not the same, due to the psychological and economic distortions introduced by racial discrimination. In fact, these beliefs were important in the decision to stratify students by race.

Nevertheless, while direct comparisons of the parameters do not seem useful, comparisons of the overall specification of family factors in the white and black models are worthwhile. With blacks as with whites, the main interest is insuring that background characteristics are adequately measured so that model misspecification does not distort the results in the more interesting sections of the model. The SES measures included in the white models appeared to capture most of the significant dimensions in background. For blacks the same three "pure" SES variables, i.e., goods index, father's education, and average family size, were included in the model. While there are reasons to suspect that these variables do not measure the educational inputs as well in the black models as in the white models, they nevertheless appear to provide an adequate representation of the relevant family environment inputs.

Within the black community there is more concern about heterogeneity of the population with regard to the relevant background characteristics. Much of this arises from the great sectional differences of the country from the black point of view. The South has not long been away from de jure segregation of blacks, and the psychological, educational, and economic impact of the South on the black population is considerably different from that found in the rest of the country. Even though this study is confined to education in the North, these sectional differences are very important because of the strong link between the North and South through migration.[4] In 1960 three-quarters of the black household heads living in the North were born in the South (as opposed to 8 percent of the white heads of households).[5] Over and above the larger variation in background by region, the regional differences are more significant for blacks.[6] Thus, there is reason to suspect that the current SES measures used to proxy family educational environment tend to be poorer measures, i.e., prone to more error, since the population is more heterogeneous. However, a wide range of different measures of black background were used, and it was found that different specifications had little effect on the structure of the rest of the model. (The different modeling efforts will be discussed in more detail below.) This leads to some optimism that any excluded dimensions of family background are uncorrelated with the included school factors and, thus, that the parameters in the more interesting section of the model are not biased by any such errors.

Many previous studies would suggest special elements of the black family structure that would call for different specification of the black background variables. In particular the controversial analysis by Daniel P. Moynihan suggests that some measure of family stability is important. He states: "There is no one Negro problem. There is no one solution. Nonetheless, at the center of the tangle of pathology is the weakness of the family structure."[7] Moynihan is neither the only one nor the first to suggest the strong influence of family structure.[8] Also, the data on black and white differences in structural integrity are compelling; over 20 percent of the urban black families exist without the husband being present, as compared with 8 percent for whites.[9]

These arguments suggest that family structure is an important dimension of black family background and should be included in the model of the educational process. Also, the use of father's education is possibly unjustified. Nevertheless, various attempts to include different family attributes and structure in the educational model failed. Variables measuring presence of father or male adult were insignificant. Also, different family education variables (mean mother's education and mean highest education of parents) added little to the overall model. Thus, even though the estimates for the father's education were quite imprecise with a t-statistic of 1.2, this formulation was retained to facilitate comparisons with the white models. The model offers no confirmation of the hypothesis of detrimental influences on education due to family instability.

The issue of family composition does raise additional doubts about the naive modeling of average family size. Certainly the implications of two adults and three children differ from those for one adult and four children. As suggested, such errors would be much more prevalent in black rather than white models. Nevertheless, average family size proves to be very significant with a coefficient three times the size of its standard error. Additionally, the magnitude of the parameter and its significance level remained unchanged in the presence of the different measures of structural integrity. Previously two hypotheses about the negative influence of family size were mentioned. Different family structures have opposite effects on the cost of living and the attention paid to children. This interaction might lessen the effect of errors due to different structures.

It does not seem profitable to dwell on the family background attributes of the model. There are reasons to suspect that the background measures for blacks contain more error than for whites. This arises from considerations of heterogeneity of the population and different family structure. Nevertheless, the three "pure" background measures of the goods index, the father's education, and the average family size appear to account for most of the significant dimensions of family background inputs to the educational process. The model characteristics are very stable under different specifications. The parameter estimates for the variables differ between whites and blacks, but it is not legitimate to compare these directly.

The consideration of attitude influences on educational production is very similar to that for background factors. At least in the short run, attitudes are not a key element of the model for policy purposes.[d] Even less is known about the attitude formation process than about the educational production process. More than that, the statistical complexities surrounding the possibility of a simultaneous relationship between achievement and attitudes imply that little faith should be placed in the specific parameter estimates for attitudes in the structural equation for achievement.

For these reasons, direct comparisons of black and white parameter estimates for attitude variables does not seem worthwhile. Additionally, there are good reasons to believe that the attitude measures between races are not directly comparable. Especially in the case of S, the percentage of students who believe that people like themselves don't have much chance for success, the possibility of having different meanings for blacks and whites seems high. Thus, the variables would only be nominally the same; the behavioral content would be different.

Nevertheless, the implications of different levels of attitudes are still present. For the two samples of schools, whites tend to aspire for more education and tend to be less pessimistic about their chances for success. For the "average" black school, a movement to the mean white values for the two attitude variables would result in a three percent increase in mean black achievement.[e] The uncertainty about attitude formation does make this more a descriptive figure than an area for public policy.

---

[d]In the long run, attitude change might be a policy instrument. In fact, recent movements within the black community have been aimed at changing attitudes. The main thrusts have been made at developing self-pride in the black race. The implications of this for the educational process are unknown.

[e]"Average" black school implies a school having the mean black sample values shown in table 5-3.

The Effect of Schools

The focal point of the educational production functions is the school section, for it is this set of inputs which is most amenable to educational policy decisions. Much hope is pinned on the effectiveness of the public schools in providing equal opportunities to all members of the society. However, there has been an increasing concern about the quality of education which is provided to minorities. The clearest finding of *Equality of Educational Opportunity* was the considerable difference in output levels (test scores) by race: blacks consistently score considerably lower than whites, even within the same geographic region. Many conclude from this that our schools have failed in their task by allowing such educational gaps to persist. Others imprudently carry this further and conclude that schools are incapable of altering the output levels prescribed by nonschool inputs, that is by family background. This conclusion is furthered by popular interpretations of *EEO*, which suggest schools have little effect. However, the models of the educational process presented in Eqs. 5.1 and 5.2 indicate that schools do have an effect on education.

The same three measures of school inputs found in the white models proved valuable in describing the educational process for black sixth graders. Teacher verbal ability (T), average teacher experience (E), and the percentage of black sixth graders who had a nonwhite teacher last year (NT) again represent the best teacher quality measures found in the *OE Survey* data. While it is useful to analyze quantitative black-white difference in the specific inputs to the process, the overall picture of the school impact is much more important. While many similar points were made in the last chapter, the interpretation of the school effects is so fundamental that the repetition found below appears justified.

The three variables represent the best macro quality measures available. The variables are best considered collectively rather than placing great emphasis on the literal definitions of individual variables. As such, they are very crude measures of what goes on in the schools and what factors bear directly on the student. There are many reasons to suspect substantial "errors" in measurement to exist. These "errors" arise not so much from faulty recording of teaching experience, although this type of error is plentiful, but rather the errors in measurement relate to inaccurate measurement of the conceptual inputs into the educational process. The average figures for the school are only approximations of the relevant stream of educational inputs encountered by the students. Additionally, the dimensions of measurement, e.g., teacher verbal facility, are only inaccurate thrusts at the significant dimensions of teaching. The errors in measurement imply that the estimated parameters in the model will be biased toward zero. The fact that any school factors of the form available from the *OE Survey* have a significant impact on achievement is somewhat surprising. The strength of the measured relationships is encouraging. In order to make comparisons with the white production functions, it is necessary to revert to a consideration of individual variables; nevertheless, the total picture of school influences should not be forgotten in the analysis of individual inputs into the process.

Teacher verbal ability exhibits a strong effect on VERBAL output with an estimated elasticity of .16. Thus, all other things equal, a 25 percent increase in the school level of teacher verbal ability (e.g., moving from an average of 20 to 25) corresponds to a 4 percent increase in the mean VERBAL output level of the school. In point of fact, it is not difficult to find schools within the same city which differ by more than 25 percent in teacher verbal ability. Between the central city and suburbs in the same SMSA, which may reasonably be considered one market for teachers, even greater differences can be found in school levels of teacher inputs.

The elasticity estimate for teacher verbal influence is slightly higher in the black model of VERBAL output than in the white model (.16 as opposed to .12). However, this small difference between the two is not statistically significant. The interpretation that teacher verbal facility is a specific technical dimension of teacher quality is furthered by the fact that its effect on MATH output is completely insignificant (t = 0.8 when included in the model). This is similar to the finding in the white production functions.

Teacher experience is the second teacher quality measure included in the model. The influence of experience in the black models is significantly more than in the white models. This variable, E, has an elasticity of .045 in the production of black VERBAL ability as opposed to .019 for whites. In the MATH equation the effect of experience is even more pronounced. The elasticity for blacks equals .085, compared with .016 for whites. (However, it must be remembered in comparing the black and white MATH equations that teacher verbal does not enter the black equation, but does enter the white equation.)

The issue of teacher selection could be more important in the case of teachers for black students than for white students. The "seniority right" of school selection which often comes with time in the school system could account for the increased influence of experience. Higher average experience levels in a school tend to indicate satisfied teachers, as they don't move even though they have the opportunity to do so. There are reasons to suspect that this is more important in black education, since some school systems are known to use "difficult" (read black) schools as "proving grounds" for new teachers. Also, the presence of black students is a very visible means by which teachers assess school quality. As noted in testimony before the Civil Rights Commission, "the Negro school carries with it a stigma that influences the attitudes both on the part of outsiders and on the part of parents, students, and teachers . . . "[10] Thus, it seems that, other things equal, a more experienced faculty for blacks will be more dedicated. Nevertheless, the direct measures of teachers' choice of schools proved insignificant in the models, even when the experience measure was removed from the model. This could happen even if the selection hypothesis was applicable, though. The direct measures represent strong choice (would you choose this school?) Experience could include less strong attitudes, i.e., content with the school, but not wild enthusiasm. Again, it is impossible to separate the pure experience hypothesis from the selection hypothesis. However, prior knowledge suggests that selection could be relatively more important in the black case (as compared with the white case).

The final teacher quality measure is NT, the percentage of students with a nonwhite teacher last year. This has the expected negative relationship with achievement which reflects the general lower quality of the nonwhite teacher. The elasticity estimates for blacks and whites are practically identical. However, the level of significance in the black equations is lower; instead of the very high t-statistics encountered in the white models, the parameters in the black models have t-statistics of only -1.7 and -1.3. This lowered significance level indicates lower reliability of the estimated relationship and could well result from a lower ability to differentiate between black schools by this variable. It also is consistent with a hypothesis that some black teachers know the problems faced by the black student and know how to teach to him. Thus, empathy, common backgrounds, and so forth might be enough to compensate for some quality differences. It is interesting that an average of 46 percent of the black sixth graders in each school had nonwhite teachers while only 13 percent of the white students had a nonwhite teacher. The change from 13 percent to 45 percent with a nonwhite teacher represents over a 7 percent decrease in mean school achievement. The negative effect of nonwhite teachers is a dramatic portrayal of a basic dilemma that must be confronted with "community control" of schools: finding enough quality teachers who also reflect other desirable personality and background characteristics sought by individual communities.

The picture that emerges from the analysis of the separate components of the school input vector is that blacks tend to react slightly more than whites to quality differences in school factors. Certainly the differences are small. Yet, they seem to be consistent. Experience has a significantly stronger influence on blacks than on whites. Teacher verbal ability displays a slightly stronger impact on blacks. Finally, the influence of nonwhite teachers, the measure of the lower ranges of teacher quality, is the same for blacks and whites. The errors in variables lead to some doubts about the general reliability of the point estimates of the parameters. However, there is little reason to believe that the errors would introduce greater bias in the white equations than in the black equations.[f] The evidence on specific differences between the black and white process with

---

[f] It is possible that the poorer measure of background characteristics contributes to the measured differences between blacks and whites. This would arise if there were significant errors in the background measures that were correlated with school quality. This source of bias does not seem extremely important since the background measures for blacks appear adequate.

respect to schools is quite circumstantial. However, differential impacts of the vector of school inputs or various components are important policy concerns. If various components have different influences, a simple redistribution of teaching personnel might yield significant gains in total educational output. Also, it might indicate special characteristics of teachers which were advantageous in ghetto schools.

Racial Composition

The final aspect of the educational production functions is the racial composition of the school. It is not surprising that the racial composition effects in the educational production functions differ between black and white. While the method of modeling racial composition is similar, both the estimates and the interpretation of the parameters differ between races. Thus, this section breaks from the comparative mode of analysis.

The racial composition of the school in the black model is measured by two variables, N_{45-75} and N_{75-100}. These variables equal the percentage black sixth graders if within the relevant range (45 to 75 percent or 75 to 100 percent) and equal zero otherwise. As noted in chapter 4, the percentage black was divided into a number of variables in order to test for differential impacts of racial composition over various ranges. The divisions were fairly arbitrary (although ranges smaller than 25 percent were analyzed, but subsequently aggregated). The use of variables in this form provides an approximation of a nonlinear function. This construction (the use of slope dummies) allows for a continuous relationship with racial composition within the given range and, thus, is conceptually superior to the use of ordinary dummy variables which merely change the intercept for different categories, but allow no variation within categories. Intercept dummy variables are insignificant in the presence of the continuous racial composition variables used.

As in the white models, racial composition variables for the entire range of schools were tested. However, only those pertaining to concentrations over 45 percent were significant. Again, it is not sensible to apply a strict interpretation to the variables. They represent approximations of a nonlinear function. Especially with the arbitrary definition of ranges, the implication that there is a sudden drop in achievement when a boundary is crossed is not realistic. A looser interpretation is better in this case.

Both racial composition variables exhibit a negative relationship with achievement. However, the estimated coefficients of $-.012$ for N_{45-75} and $-.007$ for N_{75-100} are the lowest elasticities of the eleven inputs into the educational process. Thus, there is a very small marginal effect of changing the racial composition. By a strict interpretation at the most detrimental point of racial composition (75 percent black) the mean educational output for blacks is, ceteris paribus, 95 percent of the level for a school with less than 45 percent black sixth graders. At other levels of racial composition, the achievement effects are less.

It is likely that these estimated parameters are actually greater (in absolute value) than the true value, i.e., that the estimates are biased away from zero. This conclusion is a result of a priori knowledge that there is often a considerable amount of internal segregation in schools. Internal racial division results from both overt policies and such magnificent segregators as tracking or grouping by ability. If internal segregation exists, the effective or true percentage is greater than the measured percentage black. This systematic error component will lead to overstating the racial composition parameters, and, thus, the estimates in Eqs. 5.1 and 5.2 appear to be outside limits for the true effect of racial composition.

There are several reasonable interpretations of the total racial composition relationship, and the data are insufficient to differentiate among them. The overall relationship is consistent with the observation that black schools often receive less school resources. It is possible that percentage black in a school is a good measure of overall school quality. The racial composition of the school is also a good measure of many neighborhood and community factors. Higher concentrations of blacks are systematically related to worse housing conditions, higher unemployment rates, and a series of community conditions which undoubtedly affect the school experiences of the black child. Finally, there could be a "pure" segregation effect, i.e., that racial isolation in schools per se leads to lower achievement. While more will be said about this last explanation in chapter 6, two general comments can be made at this point. First, it is not possible to separate the different factors which go into the negative relationship between high concentrations of blacks and achievement. However, it is likely that the relationship includes elements of all three. Second, the combination of the three different elements is quite small, indicating that the independent contribution of any one factor is minute.

The coefficients for the two ranges are quite close.[g] Still, the differences are interesting enough that they are presented separately (though doubts about the actual magnitude of difference remain). If this is a fair picture of the production process, racial composition has no effect on black achievement until about half of the student body is black. After that point, mean black achievement is lower. However, when a school is over three-quarters black the detrimental effect is not as great. Again a literal interpretation of the function is unwarranted. It is the general U shape of racial composition that is interesting.

There are two plausible explanations for the differential impact over these two upper ranges. The added disadvantage in the mid-range could be a reflection of dynamic factors at work. Racial compositions in this range may signify

---

[g]In the VERBAL equation, the t-statistic for the null hypothesis that the coefficients are identical equals 1.5. In the MATH equation, the t-statistic equals 1.04.

"transitional" neighborhoods which are moving from white to black. Increased tensions are certainly a symptom of the much observed "tipping" of neighborhoods. This could lead to the lowering of educational attainment during the period of change. A second explanation is more speculative. If teachers tend to "teach to whites" until the point where blacks are the overwhelming majority, this differential effect would be possible. This assumes that, when the class is all black, teachers make an effort to relate school to the black experience. It has often been suggested that efforts in this direction would improve the achievement of disadvantaged children; however, it is not known if this mode of teacher behavior was found in the sample.

More information than is available in the sample is needed to separate these hypotheses. Knowledge about dynamic community characteristics and/or detailed information on classrooms is needed. For policy purposes it would be valuable to know which factor was dominant, for each suggests quite different policies. In particular, the latter hypothesis—that teacher methods bring about improved performance—has implications for the borrowing by central cities of "new and improved" methods and curricula developed in the progressive suburban systems. Instead more localized solutions are called for.

In summary, the influence of racial composition on black education is complex. The results are consistent with several quite different hypotheses, and with the available data it is not possible to distinguish between the various hypothesized relationships. Nevertheless, one point is clear: The combined effect of the different factors measured by racial composition is small. Moreover, there are reasons to suspect that the estimates are actually biased upward.

Miscellany

In the white production functions the lack of good facility measures did not seem too damaging. Within the general range of facilities in the white sample, the expectations of direct effects of plant and equipment are not very large. Even so, the available data on facilities are insufficient to provide reasonable tests of facility effects on white achievement.

For modeling black achievement, the data are no better. However, there is reason to be more concerned about this lack of information for black models. To the extent that facilities bring physical discomfort, are poorly lighted or have no soundproofing, it is necessary to modify the basic model which specifies that facilities don't enter directly into achievement. In other words, at the lower end of the distribution of facilities there is a higher probability that facilities are an important argument of the production function. Given that ghetto schools tend to be older and less well maintained, it is more probable that facilities are directly important in producing achievement. As shown in Table 5-4, blacks in northern metropolitan areas attend older schools and schools with more

Table 5-4

Facility Characteristics of Elementary Schools for Blacks and Whites—Metropolitan Northeast and Midwest

	Northeast		Midwest	
	Black	White	Black	White
Percentage of students in schools which are:				
less than 20 years old	31%	59%	28%	63%
20 to 39 years old	23	23	18	18
40 or more years old	43	18	53	18
Average number of makeshift rooms per building	1	0	1	0

Source: *Equality of Educational Opportunity*, p. 68.

makeshift rooms.[h] Most striking is the comparison between blacks and whites for percentage attending schools over forty years old. The measure of classroom age does not have a significant effect on achievement, but this does not relieve the concern. The variance in renovations and maintenance seems large enough to obscure an age-achievement relationship. We can only conclude that the chance for error due to facility effects seems higher in the black models.

The Education of Blacks

The necessity of analyzing individual components of the educational process tends to obscure the overall picture. The school production functions for black education are qualitatively very similar to those for white education. Both appear to be fair attempts at estimating a statistical model of the educational process. The educational process is extremely complex, and the models here are highly simplified versions of elementary education. Nevertheless, they provide several useful insights into the process.

The clearest point in both the black and the white models is that schools definitely have a significant effect on achievement. Using very crude measures of the teaching staff, it was discovered that there are rewards in terms of better education if the teacher quality is raised. In comparing the black and white models of the process, it appears that blacks are more sensitive than whites to changes in quality of teachers. These differences are small, but the total impression is one where schools have a larger impact on blacks. This is an

---

[h]The work with the raw data from the *OE Survey* required for this analysis leads to some doubts about the information on makeshift rooms, as there was a fairly large nonresponse problem with this and very little information by which this could be estimated. These data on makeshift rooms are included from *EEO* with reservations.

interesting finding given the evidence that schools don't have much effect on Mexican-Americans. The present finding suggests that the Mexican-American finding is not simply a minority problem. Additionally, the larger effect of experience indicates that, in the case of blacks, school hiring policies are not as inefficient as in the case of whites. However, the coefficient is not large enough to suggest that the present large premiums paid for experience are entirely justified.

Finally, high concentrations of blacks are associated, ceteris paribus, with lower black achievement. At this point, we merely note that this simple finding belies the complexity of the actual situation. The measured effect is very small, and even that is probably biased upward.

Race and Public Education

Few public issues are so emotionally charged as that of school desegregation, few so wrapped in confusion and clouded with misunderstanding. None is more important to our national unity and progress.[1]

These were the words of President Richard Nixon in his policy statement on school desegregation, and they couldn't be more accurate. Nothing is more certain of evoking interest in school board meetings or school board elections than a discussion of school desegregation. In fact, past discussions of school desegregation have led to the development of a code language. For example, "busing" no longer refers to a means of transporting people; instead it is taken by a large number of people to imply a degradation of school quality and an obviously detrimental educational policy. And, "neighborhood schools" ranks next to "no taxation without representation" as a rallying phrase for the population. However, all of the emotional reactions have not led to better understanding of the implications of school desegregation.

One of the most significant changes in recent civil rights history has been the shift in interest from the South—the traditional home of segregation and discrimination—to the North—the bastion of civil liberties. And, while the terminology is somewhat changed (with de facto segregation replacing de jure segregation), the concerns are the same. These concerns can partially be addressed within this study, since considerable care has been given to analyzing racial aspects of Northern education. This chapter is designed to clarify how the previous chapters relate to desegregation policies. However, as will soon become apparent, much of the problem of school segregation and education remains outside of the purview of this study.

Before addressing the relationship between the previous evidence on education and desegregation policy, a conceivably important facet of desegregation which cannot be judged within the previous framework must be considered. Educational production relationships of the type discussed in this book cannot address the politics of resource allocation. The production functions describe feasible outputs from a set of inputs, but say nothing about the levels of inputs. If educational resources are distributed according to political power and political power is correlated with race or socioeconomic status, segregation in schools implies the possibility of educational discrimination. Thus, even if race or social status per se has no effect on educational output, desegregation in schools and classrooms could improve the education of minorities. The question is one of heterogeneity of school inputs, not of educational relationships according to racial composition of schools.

However, we have very little information on the subject of distribution of school inputs. One of the largest failings of the *OE Survey* was the inability to describe accurately the relative amounts of school inputs available to students of different races, ethnic groups and socioeconomic levels.[2] There is some scanty evidence of the racial distribution of teachers by experience and education. However, this is not very interesting if these attributes aren't important in education.

The differential availability of resources by racial group has been the subject of considerable recent judicial review. Within individual jurisdictions, there have been court cases in a number of cities—for example, Washington, D.C., Denver, Richmond, and Detroit—which relate to systematic differences in school inputs by race. These cases, argued under the Fourteenth Amendment of the Constitution and partially following the 1954 decision in *Brown v. Board of Education*, relate to both de jure segregation and to unequal teachers and facilities within the given city. Thus the political question of input distribution is deeply embedded in the judicial system, and this discussion merely recognizes the existence of these cases without going into detail about them.

An implication of the political power argument is that homogenizing the student body characteristics will homogenize the inputs to differing groups of students. Yet, as long as desegregation is considered within current political jurisdictions, the potential for equating inputs by desegregation may be limited. The concentration of minorities within central cities and the propensity for suburbs to purchase more school inputs implies a continued differential in resources by race, ethnic group, and social class.

The overall availability of resources to different cities has itself been the subject of a new set of court challenges. Beginning with a California Supreme Court decision (*Serrano v. Priest*) in the fall of 1971, a number of different courts have held that support of schools by local property taxes is unconstitutional as it discriminates against individuals on the basis of wealth. The logic of these rulings is discussed elsewhere, but even the final judicial opinion on this type of action is not available yet.[3] For our purposes here, it is sufficient to note the major implication of such rulings: it has led to considerable discussion of various equalizing schemes to reduce the variance in the amount of expenditures for education across different jurisdictions.[4] These actions may ameliorate the expenditure differences, although the outcome is currently very uncertain. (And, as discussed elsewhere, the effect of expenditure equalization on the distribution of educational outputs is also quite uncertain.)

Apart from political considerations in input distribution is the argument that racial composition enters explicitly into the production functions for education. In other words, for a given student background and set of school inputs, the argument states that the racial composition of the school affects the achievement of the student. This argument, with a major qualification, falls within the purview of this analysis of educational production functions.

The qualification involves not the technique of analysis but the measure of outputs. The most compelling arguments for desegregation fall in the socialization dimension of output—not the cognitive. This chapter first outlines the socialization arguments and then presents the cognitive effect evidence. Finally, a discussion of the policy implications for desegregated education is presented.

The Problem—Socialization Aspects

The term de facto segregation signifies racial isolation which results from sources other than school segregation laws or policies. In 1954 the U.S. Supreme Court ruled that de jure segregation, the explicit assignment of pupils to schools by reason of race, was unconstitutional. Yet, in northern metropolitan areas discrimination in the housing market and neighborhood schools, with frequently gerrymandered attendance lines, yield much the same picture as de jure segregation, only the name and the legal status is different. In Washington, D.C., 90 percent of the blacks attend schools that are over 90 percent black; in Gary, 89 percent attend black schools; in Cleveland, 82 percent; in Philadelphia, 72 percent.[5] In fact, as shown in table 6-1, in 1968, for all elementary and secondary schools, over three-quarters of all blacks were in schools with over half minority students, and, indeed, over 60 percent were in schools with over

Table 6-1

Distribution of Black Students by Minority Enrollment in Public Elementary and Secondary Schools, 1968

	Total	North and West[a]	Border[b]	South[c]
Percentage of Black Students by Minority enrollment of Schools:				
Under 50%	23.4	27.6	28.4	18.4
80-100%	68.0	57.4	63.8	78.8
100%	39.7	12.3	25.2	68.0

[a]Alaska, Ariz., Calif., Colo., Conn., Idaho, Ill., Ind., Iowa, Kans., Maine, Mass., Mich., Minn., Mont., Neb., Nev., N.H., N.J., N. Mex., N.Y., N. Dak., Ohio, Oreg., Pa., R.I., S. Dak., Utah, Vt., Wash., Wis., Wyo.

[b]Del., D.C., Ky., Md., Mo., Okla., W. Va.

[c]Ala., Ark., Fla., Ga., La., Miss., N.C., S.C., Tenn., Texas, Va.

Source: U.S. Bureau of the Census, *Statistical Abstract of the United States, 1971*, p. 117.

95 percent minority students. Additionally current population trends indicate that central cities are becoming blacker as black in-migrants replace whites who are moving from the central cities to the suburbs. Thus, the further concentration of blacks in black schools seems assured.

The following discussion presents no new analysis of the relationship between racial composition of schools and socialization aspects of schooling. Instead it attempts to acknowledge a considerable amount of diverse research which bears on the subject and to present a cameo of suggestive findings developed elsewhere. And, in that attempt it is admittedly too cryptic to be fully satisfying for anyone desiring an in-depth review of such information; most of the flavor of the analyses and controversy over findings has been eliminated. Nevertheless, the message is easily stated: There are many important effects of segregation in schools and society which cannot be neglected.

Concern about segregated education arises from a belief that such a racial division engenders many detrimental effects for minority children. Many psychological effects on the black have been documented. Segregated education has a significant and presumably harmful effect on black attitudes. The *OE Survey* itself indicates a considerable difference in attitudes between blacks and whites in "fate" control with almost twice as many blacks as whites in the metropolitan North believing that luck is more important than hard work and that they don't have much of a chance for success.[6] Further, these attitudes within the black population appear to be adversely affected by having fewer white classmates.[7] Black children who grow up in the ghetto and attend black schools are ill-prepared to participate in the essentially white society where their future jobs are found. They are uneasy in dealing with whites; they are distrusting of whites; and they tend to be antagonistic toward whites.[8] These psychological aspects are summarized by the Group for the Advancement of Psychiatry.

Whenever segregation occurs, one group, in this instance the Negroes, always suffers from inferior social status. The damaging effects of this are reflected in unrealistic inferiority feelings, a sense of humiliation, and constriction of potentialities for self-development. This often results in a pattern of self-hatred and rejection of one's own group, sometimes expressed by antisocial behavior toward one's own group or the dominant group. These attitudes seriously affect the levels of aspiration, the capacity to learn, and the capacity to relate in interpersonal situations.[9]

The existence of de facto segregation also has a direct bearing on future jobs of blacks as the general lack of background variance in black schools limits occupational aspirations. A statement about ghetto students before the Civil Rights Commission offers an adequate summary. "They didn't think that they could do anything because their fathers had common labor jobs and they didn't think they could ever get any higher and they didn't work, some of them."[10]

The probability of obtaining job information is also lowered; the ways of gaining information about occupations and specific jobs are such (generally from friends or relatives) that the restricted nature of the schooling experience cannot help but have lasting effects.[11]

The benefits from reducing the extent of de facto segregation are not restricted to the black community. The civil disorders of 1966 and 1967 provided dramatic evidence that society as a whole would benefit from more amicable race relations and better understanding between blacks and whites. Corrections of distortions in the job market would yield additional benefits.

The psychological impact of racial isolation in the schools also do not appear limited solely to the minority student. White students, isolated in the suburbs, are not free from the effects of racial isolation, since they must enter a society in which the racial element is very much present. Dr. Kenneth Clark has labeled the psychological implications to whites as "moral schizophrenia."[12]

The essential point to be made about de facto segregation in the schools is that the issues are very fundamental to our society. There are many broad reasons for believing that de facto segregation has a detrimental effect on minority students and society as a whole. These reasons led the Kerner Commission to conclude in their discussion of schools:

We have seen in this last summer's disorders the consequences of racial isolation, at all levels, and of attitudes toward race, on both sides, produced by three centuries of myth, ignorance, and bias. It is indispensable that opportunities for interaction between the races be expanded. "The problems of this society will not be solved unless and until our children are brought into a common encounter and encouraged to forge a new and more viable design of life."[13]

While the magnitude of costs arising from de facto segregation is unknown, the fragmentary evidence presented suggests that they could be considerable.

It is difficult to predict exactly what aspects of socialization would be affected by school integration and how much any effect might be. The past research on this is somewhat fragmentary and, thus, it is only possible to give some general views and impressions.[14] Nevertheless, this is clearly the place to look for a majority of the effects from desegregation.

The Narrow Analysis of Segregation

In any empirical analysis of de facto or de jure segregation the measurement of output is crucial. The previous analysis of educational production functions used test scores as a measure of educational output on the grounds that these were highly correlated with future incomes and success in society. However, in studying the effects of racial composition on output, this choice does not seem nearly as reasonable. The issues involved in school segregation are much more fundamental than the technical dimension measured by achievement scores. It is unreasonable a priori to expect racial composition to have a major effect on verbal skills.

Even so, considerable weight has been attached to investigations of de facto segregation in the dimension of verbal ability scores. *EEO* has been interpreted as providing a case for integration through its analysis of verbal ability and racial composition. But, probably the most influential document in this area is the Civil Rights Commission report, *Racial Isolation in the Public Schools*, a second document using *OE Survey* data on verbal ability to analyze integration. While this latter report does a good job of identifying various dimensions of the de facto segregation problem, it relies almost entirely upon analysis of the narrow output measure (verbal scores) for empirical support in its plea for remedial action. The claim made is that the racial composition of the school exerts a strong, independent effect on black students' achievement. This analysis has been widely quoted and appears to have had considerable influence. Finally, more recent re-analyses of the *OE Survey* data have followed in the same path—looking at desegregation gains in terms of verbal achievement—and, thus, have helped solidify this mode of discussion.[15]

School integration is an important and controversial area of public policy, and, since emphasis has been placed on achievement aspects of de facto segregation, it is profitable to review the evidence in this area. The production functions previously presented offer some evidence about the effects of racial composition. The major effort in this section will be to relate the mode of analysis in *Racial Isolation* to the previously estimated models of the educational process. The findings presented there and in similar studies can best be considered through such a comparison.

The primary objective of this section is suggesting relevant analyses for desegregation questions. This involves insuring: (1) that the entire case for integration is not couched in terms of the narrow questions of achievement effects; and, (2) that inappropriate evidence does not become the basis for desegregation discussions. A demonstration of adverse achievement effects from de facto segregation might provide good supporting evidence for an integration case. However, it is not the entire case. And, further, by itself it does not indicate the appropriate decision.

Incomplete Models of Education

Many logically separable issues are often confused in discussions of de facto segregation and education. When it is observed that minority group children in segregated schools score lower on achievement tests, it cannot be concluded that segregated education per se caused the output differences. Such lower achievement could come from different levels of family inputs (a cultural deprivation hypothesis), from inferior school inputs (a discrimination or lack of political power hypothesis), from segregated education being inherently detrimental, or from a combination of the three. The above distinctions are more than semantical distinctions for, if the objective is simply raising achievement, each cause calls for different remedial action. Background deficiencies call for improvement in minority family education and attitudes, compensatory education, or programs to lessen family influence, e.g., Headstart or longer school days. Poorer school inputs obviously call for input equalization. Inherent inequities of school segregation call for integration plans of some sort; for example, busing or open attendance districts. A mixture of causes probably calls for a mixture of remedies.[16]

The components for an analysis of racial composition which are suggested by the various concerns are very similar to the vectors of inputs into the conceptual model of the educational process (Equation 2-1). In fact, analysis of the independent effects of racial composition on achievement is best done within the framework of the production function for education since this allows a separation of the various aspects of the problem. There are two issues to be considered: 1) the correspondence of the production function analyses and the type of analysis in *Racial Isolation* and 2) the implications for integration of the production functions of chapters Four and Five.

The link between the production function analysis and the presentation in the Civil Rights Commission report is not always easy to make. Yet, establishing the correspondence is a precondition to demonstrating the analytic problems surrounding its discussion of integration in the narrow framework of verbal ability. Since *Racial Isolation* is so widely cited and since its mode of analysis has reoccurred frequently, it is important to understand what can be inferred from its analytical framework.

Racial Isolation bases the majority of its conclusions on an analysis of the *OE Survey* data and, primarily, the data for *twelfth grade students* in the metropolitan Northeast. The production functions of chapters 4 and 5 were estimated for *sixth grade schools* in a somewhat larger metropolitan North region.[a] The different regional coverages do not appear very serious as one would expect this to be a fairly homogeneous group of states. However, the different grade levels for the analyses and the difference between individual and school production functions could be serious, since the discussion in chapter 4 about errors introduced by both factors holds with equal force now. Some difference could be introduced by the different grade levels due to substantive differences in integration effects (as opposed to the historical errors of measurement discussed earlier). However, if there is a strong relationship between racial composition and achievement, there is little reason to believe that its effects are qualitatively different between the sixth and twelfth grades. (Many people hypothesize that

---

[a]The additional states in the production function analysis are Indiana, Illinois, Michigan, Ohio, and Wisconsin.

the impact of segregation is strongest in younger children; thus, one could expect that isolating racial composition effects would be easier and more conclusive in the sixth grade.)

A final difference between the analyses lies in the analytical methods. *Racial Isolation* rests its conclusions on a series of models of education which are analyzed through contingency tables. Such tables represent nonparametric tests of a set of hypotheses about the educational process. The various attributes of the model under consideration are divided into discrete intervals (e.g., whether average parents' education level in a school is above or below high school). Different attributes are then cross-tabulated, and mean verbal scores for the individuals in the different cells are computed. Such a nonparametric analysis does not require specifying a particular relationship, and one of the greatest virtues of this technique is its simplicity. Such an easily understood method makes it possible for a larger audience to consider the analysis than if other techniques in the realm of multivariate statistics are used. However, three aspects of contingency tables are important. First, information is lost through the division of variables into discrete intervals. Second, it is very difficult to determine more than the direction of effect. Third, it is extremely difficult to test more than a two- or three-dimensional hypothesis. Since it is possible to approximate different functional forms in multivariate regression analysis, the advantages of the parametric production function estimation seem overwhelming. Thus, the chosen strategy for linking the previous production function estimates to the results presented in *Racial Isolation* was the estimation of the models used in the Civil Rights Commission analysis within the production function framework.

The Commission tests a series of two- and three-dimensional models of the educational process and supports most of its conclusions by such an analysis of achievement. The central conclusion in *Racial Isolation*, and the one most important for this section is: "In addition to these factors [family background, school inputs, and peers], the racial composition of schools appears to be a distinct element. Racial isolation tends to lower students' achievement . . ."[17] The primary model which is used to support this conclusion "controls for" student and school social class and presents average achievement levels for blacks under different racial mixes.[18] It is this basic model which was re-analyzed within the production function framework for the 242 schools with black sixth graders. Equation 6.1 is a simple linear regression model of mean verbal achievement of black sixth graders. Equation 6.2 is a log-log model with the same variable specification. These may be considered more sophisticated tests of the models in *Racial Isolation*. Three measures of social class are used: G is the goods index for the school, E_f is mean father's education, and FS is mean family size. The variable of interest in this analysis is N, the percentage of sixth graders who are black.[19] All variables are allowed to be continuous over the relevant range of values, and estimation was accomplished using ordinary least squares (unweighted).

$$\text{VERBAL} \quad = 2.61 + .310 + .101E_f - .358FS - .028N$$
$$(.9) \quad (12.6) \quad (1.0) \quad (-1.1) \quad (-4.1)$$

$$SE = 3.10 \qquad R^2 = .46 \tag{6.1}$$

$$\text{VERBAL*} \quad = -.78 + .769G* + .035E_f* - .094FS* - .046N*$$
$$(-2.0) \quad (12.8) \quad (1.8) \quad (-1.4) \quad (-4.2)$$

$$SE = .13 \qquad R^2 = .45 \tag{6.2}$$

---

*Asterisks indicate logarithms of variables. t-statistics are found below each coefficient. *SE* is the standard error of the regression (unweighted ordinary least squares).

The equations represent two alternative specifications of the racial composition effect measured by N, the percentage black in the school. While other forms of the racial mix variable were tested, there was little indication that any other form was more appropriate. In the presented equations, the racial composition coefficient is over four times its standard error. The models imply that, holding the effects of socioeconomic background constant, higher black achievement is associated with lower proportions of black students. It is difficult to compare the production function estimate directly to the contingency table analysis of *Racial Isolation*.[20] However, the qualitative impressions are very similar. Equations 6.1 and 6.2 both imply significant and strong effects of integration over and above the influence of social class.

Does this imply that the case for integration has been established? It does not! Equations 6.1 and 6.2 are nothing more than misspecifications of the previously presented models of the educational process. When a complete model of the educational process is analyzed, one returns to the results presented in Eq. 5.1. This equation, the production function for black sixth graders, contains a number of insights into Eqs. 6.1 and 6.2 and the whole issue of de facto segregation. First, in the modeling efforts of chapter 5 it was discovered that racial composition was only important in the higher ranges of percentage black (greater than 45 percent). Additionally, the magnitude of the effects were very small. In the log-log model of Eq. 5.1 (which is comparable to Eq. 6.2), the estimated elasticities were −.012 in the range 45 to 75 percent black and −.007 for greater than 75 percent black. The estimated effect in the *Racial Isolation* model (−.046) is four times the maximum value found in the complete model.[21] And, there were doubts expressed in chapter 5 as to whether the true value was really as large as the estimated parameter.

It is obvious what has happened. In the misspecified models presented in *Racial Isolation*, the racial composition of the school does a good job of proxying school quality. When school inputs are included in the model of the educational process, racial composition only enters in a very special manner (with slope dummies for higher ranges of percentage black), and the apparent effect of racial composition is considerably reduced. As expressed previously, there are also some interpretative problems associated with this effect since racial composition tends to act as a good surrogate for several other inputs to the process.

A final note on the use of test score justifications for integration is necessary. When reliance is placed on this dimension, closer attention must be paid to the structure of benefits from integration. In particular, the most fundamental returns to integration (mainly attitudes and interracial experience) appear positive for both blacks and whites. However, it is conceivable that this is not the case for technical output and that integration is more like a zero sum game with whites losing what blacks gain. In fact, if one uses the same simple model of racial composition effects that was used in *Racial Isolation* for whites, there is a definite negative effect of integration.[22] In a linear estimate of VERBAL achievement for whites as a function of the three "pure" SES factors and percentage black sixth graders, the percentage black variable had a statistically significant ($t = -6.3$) negative effect on white achievement. Additionally, the estimated parameter of $-.041$ is larger than the corresponding parameter in Eq. 6.1. Thus, naively interpreted, it appears that white mean ahievement is lowered by more than black mean achievement is raised if racial compositions are adjusted. (Similar results hold for a logarithmic form of the white equation.) However, the more complete models in chapter 4 portray a different picture. The most reasonable interpretations of Eqs. 4.1 and 4.2 (the complete white models) indicate that no evidence of detrimental integration effects was found. In the VERBAL equation, but not the MATH equation, high concentrations of blacks (over 75 percent) were negatively related to achievement. However, this is best thought of as a mixture of poor school quality and an extreme of the white SES distribution. The simple white models do demonstrate the dangers of naive reliance on misspecified models.

The point of this entire section is simple. It seems imprudent to defend integration in the very narrow terms of verbal ability test scores. The educational production functions for black sixth graders presented in the previous chapter considered the effects of racial composition on achievement. With even the most charitable interpretation, the independent effects of de facto segregation on black achievement are modest; large integration effects are only found in misspecified models of the educational process. The arguments for integration are much more fundamental than any effects on verbal learning, and, by overemphasizing this narrow analysis, the chances of discrediting the entire case are high.

A Qualification

The fact that integration per se does not have a strong effect on verbal achievement does not tell the entire story. It is plausible that positive school peer effects exist for individuals, i.e., better student bodies have a positive effect on individual students. It is not possible to test this hypothesis with the *OE Survey* data.[23] However, on the assumption that this effect exists, a better case for integration using verbal ability score evidence might be made.

The peer group hypothesis is usually stated that lower-class children benefit from being in schools with middle- and upper-class children, and that these middle- and upper-class children do not suffer. The obvious implication of this hypothesis is that social class integration in schools is a net gain to society, for nobody loses but some gain.

However, the factor of race confounds the situation. It is not feasible to achieve social class integration within the black community. By any reasonable standard, no more than a third of the black families could be considered middle class or upper class. Thus, if social class integration is the goal, racial integration must be undertaken. To the extent that racial integration brings social class integration, the peer group hypothesis suggests a consequent gain in achievement scores of the blacks.

Nevertheless, it still seems unprofitable to judge the gains of integration by points of verbal ability. While the gains due to peer influences brought about through racial integration might be significant, the most pervasive reasons for integration are still found elsewhere. Peer effects cannot be analyzed with the *OE Survey* data and, thus, no statements about this aspect of integration can be within the multisystem analysis.

The data in chapter 3 do pertain directly to peer influences. The models in that chapter indicate that peer influences, as measured by either the occupational distribution or ethnic distribution of classrooms, do not affect third grade achievement. Even though the Mexican-American distribution within a classroom ranged from virtually none to two-thirds of the class, the remaining white students were unaffected. The same holds for occupational distribution and for differences in entering achievement levels.

One remaining qualification stands out. All of the analysis has concentrated upon elementary education. It could well be that any peer effects—especially those working through attitude formation—would not show up until later grades. Nevertheless, most of the heated debate over neighborhood schools, busing, etc., centers on elementary schools.

Desegregation and Educational Policy

Many issues of educational policy are internal to the schools and do not require an analysis which explicitly considers society as a whole. For example, efficiency in hiring teachers does not require consideration of the neighborhood housing conditions for students. However, desegregation policy is an example of policy which cannot be made without explicit consideration of the interdependencies of school and society at large.

Segregation and discrimination are elements of many facets of our society. They exist not only in our schools but in housing; in labor markets; in recreational facilities. Earl Raab describes the interrelationships as follows:

The vicious circle of low economic status, ghettoized housing, segregated schools, sub-standard school achievement, leading back to low economic status, tends to retard integration and equal achievement, even where discrimination and formal segregation are on the decrease.[24]

Many people have hypothesized that the school is the point to break into this vicious circle and change its path. Further, many believe that the way to do this is necessarily through school desegregation.

The appropriate calculations—the weighing of benefits and costs—for various school desegregation plans clearly does not rest solely on the determination of whether or not the racial composition of a school affects achievement. And, the resolution of the issues involved relies as much on hunch, philosophy, and goals as it does on scientific evidence about the educational process. Since these are areas not easily addressed within the restricted framework of the previous data and analyses, they are best left until the final chapter, which more explicitly incorporates outside information into the discussion of educational policy.

7 Summary and Beyond

The central thesis of this book has been that educational policy decisions cannot be made *in vacuo*. Policy concerns about the outputs of the educational process can only be addressed through knowledge about the relationship between the inputs and the outputs of the educational process. This arises from the simple fact that policy makers can affect outputs only indirectly; educational output by itself can neither be purchased in the market nor be willed higher by the policy maker.

Yet, the pivotal role that educational input-output relationships conceptually should play in decision making should not be interpreted as implying that they are, in reality, important. The reason: very little is known about them. Educators have traditionally professed to know what the production relationships look like in education, at least within certain bounds. Their notions, however, have been increasingly questioned. Both public and judicial dissatisfaction with the outcomes and with the expense of the educational system have occasioned a reappraisal of traditional educational methods. This reappraisal, conducted within the general framework of educational production relationships, has not exonerated the educators, but, to the contrary, has added support to many of the fundamental attacks on the educational system.

This concluding chapter first summarizes the major empirical findings of the set of systematic inquiries into the educational process developed in this study. It then delves into the implications of these raw findings. The implications are somewhat pretentiously labeled "policy implications," although it is best to think of them as illustrative extensions of the empirical work. There is an enormous amount of uncertainty surrounding the findings here (and elsewhere), and it would be entirely premature to act now. To paraphrase, "the media is the message." While the analyses are interesting in their own right, the questions, the mode of analysis, and the method of interpreting results are the central lessons to be gained.

The organization of both the summary and the policy sections follows directly from the introductory chapter. The question of resource allocation—that is, deciding on inputs to the educational process—is discussed first. Within this study, resource allocation really boils down to hiring and paying teachers, and in this light several alternatives are analyzed. After this, the distribution of outputs is taken up. Alternative schemes for altering the observed racial distribution of achievement are considered within the context of the previously developed models of the educational process.

The Findings

Conceptually, educational output can be thought of as a function of family inputs, peer inputs, innate abilities, and schools inputs. Within this framework, there is clearly a wide latitude for discretion, and considerable care must be exercised in the precise specification and estimation of a global model such as this one. An attempt has been made throughout the actual model development to point out and warn the consumer about particularly uncertain elements of the models presented.

The findings summarized here are derived from two separate analyses. Both analyses concentrate upon elementary education and, in particular, upon the production of achievement levels or cognitive ability. The first analysis (chapter 3) develops models within a single California school system for individual student value added, or additions to achievement, in the second and third grades. The second analysis (chapters 4 and 5) delves into total school achievement levels in the sixth grade for a sample of urban schools in the Northeast and Great Lakes regions.

The findings can be easily summarized. There is no doubt that family background has a pervasive and powerful impact on student achievement; higher socioeconomic status is systematically related to higher achievement.[1]

Past interpretations of this finding amply illustrate the pitfalls in research into the educational production process. From an educational standpoint, the important aspects of family inputs include the quantity and quality of family interactions, the attitudes and the ambitions developed, the specific "schooling" that takes place in the home, and so forth. These attributes tend to be positively correlated with socioeconomic status, and, because data measuring actual family educational inputs are generally unavailable, surrogates in the form of family income, wealth, or status are often employed to portray family differences. But, the empirical importance of these surrogates in estimated models of education does not imply that changing the level of these surrogates (say income) will have a very large, immediate effect on achievement. To the extent that the actual family inputs—interactions, attitudes, etc.—remain unchanged, achievement would be expected to remain unchanged.[a] This distinction considerably lessens public policy interest in the estimated importance of family background in explaining achievement differences. It is difficult to conceive of reasonable programs designed to change achievement by operating on the "real" family inputs. It would for instance be extremely expensive to educate the school-age

---

[a]There are a number of qualifications to this statement. First, programs to change family income such as in the proposed Family Assistance Plan may be desirable in their own right. Here we are discussing only the value of such plans as an instrument of short-run educational policy. Second, they might have some short-run educational effects at the lower extreme through the provision of adequate shelter and diet. Third, they might have some long-run effects by encouraging more investment in health and education by low income families, although it would take some time to notice these effects.[2]

population by intensively educating the adult population. (Though educating adults may be desirable for its own merits.) Alternatively, attempts to change the existing family relationships or to reduce family inputs into education seem neither politically feasible nor altogether desirable.[b]

Part of the interest in "family effects" undoubtedly relates to absolving the schools of guilt in inequality of educational opportunity. But, to the extent that the importance of family background in education is used to assess blame for low achievement by a group, there is something wrong with the way in which we are viewing schools. In terms of average outputs by racial and ethnic group, commitments to educational equality do not differentiate among sources of inequality. Public school systems supposedly have a founding in democratic principles which express a desire to reduce the intergenerational correlation of educational levels.[3] And, from a public policy viewpoint, past sources of inequality should not be the justification for future inequality.

The importance of the quantity and quality of school inputs is more interesting from a policy viewpoint than the importance of family backgrounds. The analyses indicate that differences among teachers have a significant impact upon the achievement of students. (This holds with one exception to be discussed later: Differences among schools and teachers do not appear to affect the achievement of Mexican-Americans, at least within the single system analysis of third grade education developed in chapter 3.) This general finding contradicts the broadest attacks on the public school system, namely that schools exert a homogeneous influence regardless of any resource differences.[4] It also leads to the position that achievement can be altered through proper hiring of teachers and other inputs.

Nevertheless, the results do not imply applause for the current public school system, even leaving aside for now the question of distribution of achievement outcomes among students. The overall evaluation of school resource allocation is unambiguous: schools are not operated in an efficient manner. In particular, the factors which are purchased by the school systems are not for the most part the characteristics of schools and teachers which are important in determining achievement levels.

The bulk of instructional expenditures go toward the purchase of three classes of inputs: class size, teacher experience, and teacher graduate education. None of the analyses presented in this book or in other studies supports the contention that class size or teacher graduate education influence student achievement levels. The multisystem analysis, but not the single system analysis, indicates that total teacher experience has a positive effect on achievement, but even here the contribution to achievement of increased experience is probably

---

[b]At an extreme, one could consider (mandatory?) boarding schools. Lengthening school days or school years are more limited and more feasible programs to reduce the importance of families in education; yet, given the cumulative impact of families, such programs would seem to be a small change in the family input vector.

not large enough to justify the large salary increases customarily meted out to increased experience. Thus, the findings of this research provide some guidance on what *not* to do in administering schools.

The characteristics of teachers which appear important in the estimated models include teacher verbal ability (which may also be interpreted as a measure of general intelligence), recentness of teacher educational experiences, and proportion of nonwhite teachers (which may be interpreted as a measure of the quality of the educational experiences of nonwhite teachers). However, this set of characteristics is not altogether satisfactory since hiring rules sound something like "hire good teachers." There are some practical impediments to this rule, since it is difficult to provide methods for screening teachers before they are hired. The measures for teachers are merely proxies for the attributes really desired. And, hiring on the basis of these proxies is a dubious strategy since the relationship between the proxies and the real attributes would undoubtedly change. (This is much the same as changing the proxies for family inputs). Further, what is apparent from these modeling attempts is that objective characteristics of teachers do not provide all of the information desired; much of the observed difference in teaching ability is unexplained by the simple measures used. More has to be known about the behavior of teachers, particularly behavior within the classroom. Nevertheless, even though we admittedly do not know how to measure "teaching" very well, the foregoing discussion should not be interpreted as implying that we cannot evaluate teachers *after the fact*. This will be discussed below in terms of accountability of teachers for educational performance.

These school findings implicitly say that differences in per pupil expenditures will not be systematically related to differences in student achievement. Since none of the components of expenditures have a strong effect on achievement, the aggregate of expenditures will exhibit no relationship. (This implicit finding was also directly confirmed in the multisystem analysis where a per pupil instructional expenditure variable was found to be insignificant in the estimated production functions.)[c] Thus, as will be discussed below, expenditure differences cannot be construed as differences in educational opportunity, and providing expenditure equality does not necessarily satisfy the quest for equality of educational opportunity. In fact, blind equalization of instructional expenditures within the current structure could even be counterproductive.[5]

The remaining item of interest is the effect of student body characteristics upon the education of individual children. The most intensely discussed issue is the effect of racial composition of schools upon education; however, there is

---

[c]The specific results related to actual input quantities really tell us more than the test using a per pupil expenditure variable. Differences in input price—which are known to exist—could mask the importance of the expenditure variable even in the case where real, or price adjusted, expenditures have an impact on education. The possible interpretative problems related to price differences are eliminated by looking at actual inputs.

also considerable attention paid to the social class composition of the schools. The discussion along racial lines is no stranger to public policy debates and has been a frequent visitor to the courtroom.[6] The traditional courtroom argument has been based on the equal protection clause of the 14th amendment to the U.S. Constitution with evidence for unequal schools based on differences in the inputs provided schools of different racial compositions. Recent cases have also seen the introduction of evidence on the differences in achievement or *outputs* by race in segregated schools.[7] The salient question in the context of these discussions—at least to understand the potential outcome of proposed legal remedies—relates to the effect of racial or social composition on educational outputs.

Analysis of this question indicates that, for a given set of teacher and family background characteristics, the independent effect of student body composition on achievement is small or nonexistent. Within the multischool analysis, there were noticeable effects of racial composition only in schools where there were extremely high percentages of black students.[d] The estimated effects are quite small, and, further, the nominal effects may be due more to the poor measurement of school inputs than to any race related effects. Within the single system analysis, neither racial nor social class composition of classrooms or schools impacted upon the achievement of whites or Mexican-Americans. Certainly there are many reasons to be cautious in interpreting these findings: they pertain only to cognitive development; they pertain only to elementary schools, etc. However, these findings do suggest some reevaluation of past interpretations of data and assumptions about educational production relationships.[8]

Implications for Policy—Resource Allocation

It is possible to make some *tentative* observations about the policy implications of the analyses. However, it is important to bear in mind that the conclusions are based upon a limited view of schools—limited in terms of grade levels, output measures and experiences observed. Education is extremely complex and making decisions on the basis of only the analyses here is hazardous at best. The policy implications are meant to be suggestive, and provocative, but considerably more confirmation of the results is needed.

The uncertainties about the education process are important to understand before going on to discuss policies. Within the past decade there have been perhaps two dozen major production function studies of the educational process, and they have provided amazingly few consistent findings. The differences in results—and potential policies—is documented elsewhere.[9] But an

---

[d]The percentage of the student body who were black had to be over 75 percent before white achievement was affected and over 45 percent before black achievement was affected.

illustration of the divergence of findings is perhaps useful at this point. Reanalyses of the *OE Survey* data (the data base for chapters 4-6 of this book) contained in *On Equality of Educational Opportunity* presented four separate analyses of the educational process (Jencks; Armor; Smith; and Cohen, Pettigrew, and Riley). From these studies there is a clear impression that family background is important—a finding that few people would doubt even in the absence of these studies. But the effect and interpretation of other major inputs (student body socioeconomic and racial composition, teachers and facilities) is quite ambiguous. For example, Armor argues that blacks, particularly in the South, are more sensitive than whites to differences in teacher quality while Smith and Jencks find no confirmation of this; and Cohen, Pettigrew, and Riley within their own analysis show inconclusive results for racial composition effects which are independent of the social class composition of schools. These examples, which could be continued with ease, illustrate the fragility of conclusions based on any single study.

A variety of factors could explain the lack of consistency: lack of appropriate data, differences in analytical design, varying beliefs of the researchers, etc. But the fact remains that we have a long way to go before we can have a great deal of confidence in any particular set of policies. In the end, the analyses that have been accomplished are just refined data points and must be evaluated within the context of other information about schools and education.

Hiring Teachers

The present system of hiring and paying teachers on the basis of a set of inputs is very costly. While the teacher inputs traditionally purchased (experience and graduate education) do not appear to have a strong influence on achievement, public elementary and secondary school teachers in 1970 had a median experience level of nine years, and almost 30 percent had a master's degree or more. (The distribution of teachers by experience and degree is displayed in table 7-1.)

The analyses here and elsewhere indicate that reducing teacher experience levels and the amount of teacher graduate education would have its major effect on a system's payroll while having little or no effect on student achievement. This finding offers school systems a quick way to reduce expenditures while maintaining output: Increase teacher turnover and, thereby, reduce experience levels and the concomitant expenditures. While constrained to a given salary structure, this device would promote more efficient resource allocation. Yet, even for an individual system, tenure regulations and historical rigidities would limit the effectiveness of such a policy. And, clearly, if all school systems attempted to pursue such a policy, the labor market for teachers would undoubtedly be affected and could possibly break down.

Table 7-1

Public Elementary and Secondary Schools–Percentage Distribution of Classroom Teachers, by Experience and Degrees Held: 1970

Item	Total	Elementary School	Secondary School
Teaching Experience			
1-3 years	24.0	22.0	26.1
4-6 years	18.1	15.9	20.5
7-9 years	11.1	11.7	10.6
10-14 years	15.7	15.0	16.5
15-19 years	10.2	10.7	9.6
20 years or more	20.9	24.8	16.7
Median, years	9	10	7
Highest Degree Held			
No degree	0.8	9.9	0.7
2-year degree	2.8	5.0	0.5
Bachelor's degree	65.8	72.0	59.2
Master's degree	28.6	20.5	37.2
Professional degree, 6 years	1.7	1.4	2.1
Doctor's degree	0.3	0.2	0.3

Source: U.S. Bureau of the Census, *Statistical Abstract of the United States, 1971*, p. 122.

A more appealing, long-run option might include using part of the "surplus" money, saved through a reduction in the experience-graduate education bonuses, to change the whole supply curve for teachers. The analyses here and several similar ones elsewhere support the general thesis that more intelligent teachers on average are more effective than less intelligent teachers. This finding, which is supported largely by the measures of teacher verbal facility, implies that significant changes might be induced by increasing teacher salaries relative to other occupations and, thus, increasing the average abilities of teachers.

There are, of course, other considerations in such a proposal. Certification requirements for teachers would need a thorough reexamination since they are often linked to traditional molds of teachers. Further, past tenure regulations might conflict during the transition period with attempts at seriously restructuring the pool of teachers. The reconciliation of the current stock of teachers with the desired future stock could take a number of forms: It may take a number of years to notice significant differences in the stock of teachers; it may signal the introduction of a two-salary system for new and old teachers; it may lead to windfall gains for a number of current teachers; or it may promote a variety of early retirement programs. The resolution of these issues would take time and long painful negotiations. Since the political questions and self-interests involved are all quite evident, it is not very worthwhile speculating on the possible mixture of outcomes at this time.

On the other hand, it likewise does not seem appropriate to assume that no changes are possible. For example, the McElroy Commission's report on school finance recommended increased aid to central city schools with the stipulation that none of the money could go for increased teacher salaries.[10] The clear assumption is that teacher unions would be able to bargain away all of the grants for increased salaries to current teachers. And, in the short run they are probably right that a large part of additional funds may go to such windfall gains. Yet, within the current educational technology—the one on which the analyses in the previous chapters were based—improved teachers seem to be the most reasonable way to bring about improvements in student education, and improved teachers can only be gained through changes in the salary structure.

(It is important to distinguish between local solutions and national solutions. For an individual system, it is possible to change the mix of teachers more quickly than for the nation as a whole. Individual school districts can bid more able teachers away from other districts and unilaterally appeal to a nontraditional group of potential teachers by raising teacher salaries relative to other districts and other professions. On the other hand, if all school districts in the country attempt to do this simultaneously, the outcome is less certain. There could be a severe labor market disequilibrium situation—particularly if school systems were successful in attracting people who would otherwise have entered different occupations and if traditional teacher training institutions make no adjustments in their production of potential teachers. This implies the obvious: For the nation as a whole, any attempts to change the supply function for teachers must be introduced over some length of time.)

Teacher Accountability

The level of the overall salary schedule for teachers is not the only interesting issue when considering the hiring of teachers. Clearly, the schedule must allow for differential pay to individuals and the possibility of individual advancement— otherwise the type of individual entering and remaining in teaching would be perverse. The issue of how teacher salary differentials should be set has been discussed frequently before.[11] However, two factors make the discussion more poignant now. First, the evidence about the relationship between the purchased inputs and outputs has not been well documented in the past. Thus, the argument against single salary schedules was generally made along the lines of aggregate supply of teachers or the supply of certain specialties (e.g., math and science teachers).[12] Second, the issue of accountability—holding teachers responsible for outputs—has been gaining support.[13] This would lead to setting salary differentials on the basis of outputs rather than inputs. In fact, many states have already passed laws requiring some form of accountability.

One of the most intriguing aspects of the analysis, particularly that in chapter 3, is the ability to address directly the issue of teacher accountability. The statistical models in chapter 3 provided an estimate of the relative amounts of student achievement gains that were associated with each teacher. Further, these estimates were independent of the entering achievement levels of students and the family background of students. This procedure thus allows the ranking of teachers on the basis of teaching ability, or the ability to produce student achievement, and circumvents the need to rank teachers according to surrogates for quality such as educational background. And, while some serious measurement questions still remain, they do not appear insurmountable.

The analyses here have relied upon quite limited and narrow views of outputs, and any actual applications of accountability would certainly want to broaden this range. Considerable work has already been done on this, although educational research has tended to consider only a narrow set of measures.

There are many standardized tests currently available which cover a wide variety of outputs. For example, the National Assessment of Educational Progress has developed tests for a wide range of age groups in ten subject areas: reading, writing, mathematics, social studies, citizenship, science, art, music, literature, and career and occupational development. Also considered for future use are tests in listening and speaking, consumer education, health education, physical education and study skills. These tests are an attempt to gain a more complete picture of education and to cover the different dimensions (skill and socialization) better than what has been available up until now.[14]

Also, the actual implementation of an accountability scheme would have to consider problems arising from attempts to "teach the tests." To the extent that the tests are a good sample of the desired learning outcomes, there is nothing particularly wrong with teaching the tests. And, while we may not be at a point now where we trust standardized tests to hold up under concerted attempts to foil them, conceptually the problem appears soluble. These issues are raised not because they appear insurmountable, but only because they required considerable attention before an effective accountability scheme can be introduced.

Accountability for educational outcomes is not a new idea. However, the evidence about present school inefficiency as linked to hiring and pay practices is strong motivation for considering accountability schemes. Further, the methodology here seems particularly well suited to addressing the value of individual teachers.

Implications for Policy—The Distribution of Educational Services

The analysis presented also has a direct bearing upon many of the recent questions about the distribution of educational services. The failings of the educational system in the quest for equal opportunity for racial and ethnic minorities have been the subject of so much recent attention that they do not need repeating at this point. These failings are evident both in terms of educational measures and in terms of success in society. However, even with a commitment to correct inequities, there is no consensus on what types of policies should be pursued to change the distribution.

The discussion of distributional policy options must be divided into two parts. The previous analyses are best suited to answering trade-off questions such as: Is it better to spend an additional dollar to change school student body compositions or to obtain better teachers? This may be labeled the "educational" part since it relates directly to arguments of the educational production function. However, the policy alternatives are not strictly trade-off questions because they also get into organizational matters which may affect the political feasibility of obtaining a given set of inputs. For example, does the ability to isolate poor, politically ineffective groups imply that they will systematically receive poorer school inputs? This latter part of the policy considerations, the "political" part, is not adequately handled within the framework of educational production functions but cannot be neglected. Therefore, some attempt will be made to sketch likely "political" ramifications of different policies.

This discussion will attempt to integrate the general findings of the previous analyses of the educational process with the political factors faced by public school systems. Three major policy options present themselves in discussions of changing the distribution of educational services within the current basic organization of schools: compensatory education, desegregation of schools, and community control of schools. In general, these policies should not be thought of strictly as alternatives. They tend to address different problems and different goals, and they are not mutually exclusive approaches. The choice among them will also tend to depend upon given localities. Each of the three options will be discussed separately, after which the points of potential conflict will be analyzed.

Compensatory Education

The term "compensatory education"—compensating disadvantaged children by supplying more or better school inputs—has broader connotations here than in its general usage. Most past evaluations have been concerned with specific programs—that is, types of teaching material, curriculum, teaching styles, etc.—that have been labeled compensatory. This discussion considers the "macro" possibilities of improving the achievement of lagging groups, but it does so without detailed analysis of specific programs. The exact context of improving teacher quality (curriculum and so forth) could complement or conflict with the teacher changes—thus, modifying the predicted achievement changes developed here; the program context must, of course, be considered in the "micro" application of compensatory programs to individual schools. The objective here is one of ascertaining the overall appropriateness of affecting achievement within the framework of current school operation.

The fact that teacher skills have an effect on education implies that, independent of the racial composition of the school or classroom, it is possible to improve the education of minorities through a compensatory program.[15] The amount of improvement predicted by the models is not sufficient to erase the educational gap faced by minority students—but it is not negligible as some would suggest. The teacher quality differentials observed between schools within central city school systems, weighted by their estimated importance, are equivalent to between 20 and 30 percent of the observed black-white mean verbal achievement differences in the sixth grade. And, the teacher quality differentials observed between central city and suburban schools are even larger. Such estimates, because of the poor measurement of teachers and limited range of school experiences studied, must be viewed as a lower bound on the possibility for change. (This discussion also disregards the previous policy suggestion that the pool of teachers be improved.)

This is not to say that simply supplying more money is the answer. It can be an answer only if it is used effectively. As noted throughout this study and in other studies, there appears to be no significant relationship between per pupil instructional expenditures and student achievement. This is another way of saying that, if schools operate the way they have traditionally operated, spending more money does not insure that anything will happen. For example, if a school decides to reduce its average class size from thirty to twenty students per class, it would raise instructional expenditures by close to a third and probably (according to most analyses) not affect student achievement. Yet, if it instead bought quality teachers, say on the basis of actual performance as suggested above, it could potentially raise student achievement considerably. In other words, *if schools were to act efficiently, money could be an effective instrument. But, it will take some structural changes in schools to make them operate efficiently.* Without such structural changes and presuming the same technology as currently used, more money would probably not be a solution.

School Desegregation

School desegregation is the second potential policy to alter the distribution of educational outcomes. This public policy issue—one of the most sensitive public policy issues of our time—is covered by a shroud of emotion and confusion that is hard to break through. Two points are clear, however: a majority of black and Spanish-American students attend segregated schools and, as a group, their educational achievement is less than that of white majority students. These facts are taken by some to suggest that school desegregation is a potential policy tool for improving the racial and ethnic distribution of educational outcomes and, presumably, societal outcomes.

In this area, the previous analyses in this volume are clearly insufficient as a basis of public policy. The models of the educational process, as detailed in chapter 6, relate to only cognitive development—a measure too narrow to judge appropriately the effects of school desegregation. The factors of socialization and attitudes seem more relevant.

But, for the moment, let us look at the evidence and possible relationship between school desegregation and cognitive development. The complete models of the educational process (described in chapters 3-5) suggest that there is very little gained in cognitive development from merely mixing races within schools and within classrooms. Once differences in family backgrounds and school inputs are properly allowed for, there is an insignificant independent effect of the racial composition of the school and classroom.

An important point, however, is that the quantity and quality of school inputs are not independent of the racial composition of schools. While the information is imperfect—often referring to racial differences in factors which don't seem important such as advanced degrees of teachers, a good prima facie case can be made for systematic differences in school quality. There is some, albeit small, direct evidence of school differences as in Katzman, Jencks, and Owen.[16] This evidence, not undisputed, relates to the political aspects of desegregation policies.

Further, there is indirect evidence provided by the misspecified models of achievement in chapter 6. When school factors were omitted from the estimated production functions, the effect of racial composition on achievement appeared four times as large as in the well-specified model which included school factors. The implication of this is that higher concentrations of blacks are systematically correlated with the provision of lower quality school inputs. It is, thus, important to consider the level of school inputs in conjunction with desegregation.

This conclusion does not, however, imply that simply any desegregation policy will immediately bring better school or student body inputs that will lead to improved achievement. It also does not necessarily imply that just any desegregation policy would lead to a narrowing of racial differences in achievement. For instance, imagine a large busing program for desegregation within the political boundaries of a major central city with a large minority population. One possible outcome of this is further flight of middle-class whites to suburban areas—leaving the possibilities of social class, and even racial, integration in doubt and possibly enlarging differences in average achievement for whites (now concentrated more in the suburbs) and blacks. Further imagine that the bulk of the additional costs of such busing falls upon the central city school system, leaving the school board in the unenviable position of attempting to raise taxes or decrease (nonbusing) educational inputs.[e] The distinct possibility of widened achievement disparities would again surface.

The key factor in determining the potential amount of achievement gains from a given desegregation plan is, thus, the magnitude of change in school inputs that comes from the plan. The lack of information on the variance of inputs is especially damaging here, but there is the supposition that average school quality differences within political jurisdictions (and particularly within central cities) are considerably smaller than those across different jurisdictions. This bit of conventional wisdom would suggest that desegregation "in the large"—across jurisdictional lines—would provide significantly greater achievement gains than desegregation within any given jurisdiction.

There are several possible mechanisms for introducing cross-jurisdictional desegregation. There are voluntary busing programs which take central city minority students to participating white suburban schools. An example of this type of program is Boston's METCO which, between 1966 and 1972, sent about 1,500 black students of all ages to twenty-eight surrounding communities; other examples are found in Hartford and New Haven. An alternative method of metropolitan area desegregation has been court decree. Lower courts, passing on remedies to findings of de jure segregation, have required metropolitan area busing when desegregation within central cities seems infeasible. These cases (Detroit in 1971 and Richmond in 1972) have yet to be considered by the U.S. Supreme Court, but could possibly enlarge the desegregation opportunities considerably.[17] Finally, federal and state monetary incentives could be designed to encourage voluntary school desegregation. An example of this is found in the Presidential proposal for a moratorium on mandatory busing for desegregation.[18] Each of these possible policies involves a host of sensitive political and legal issues; here it is sufficient to point out the potential gains from desegregation "in the large," without choosing among the possible mechanisms.

The consideration of differences in school inputs and school quality is more relevant for minority students than for majority students. Certainly the differences in school inputs are just as large for whites as for blacks and other minorities. However, from a public policy point of view we are not equally concerned with such school quality differences. Different people have different views on the amount of money they wish to spend on education and other things. With a system of separate local jurisdictions, each offering different public services, it is possible within limits for people to select the amount of public services, and education, which they desire through their residential

---

[e]It is difficult to ascertain how much a busing program would cost. Many school systems already do considerable busing; the only relevant costs would be the additional costs, or marginal busing expenditures, which arise from the desegregation program. It seems particularly difficult to make any generalizations in this area as costs depend upon geography, density, racial separation, etc. However, there clearly can be a significant expenditure.

location decision. (This selection with regard to any particular service is constrained by having to select "bundles" of services, making it difficult to arrive at the most desired level of any particular input). And, in such a world, neighborhood schools might be justified simply by allowing individuals to know the educational services which they will get with any given housing choice. But this is not the world faced by minorities. When restrictions on housing location exist—as amply supported elsewhere, minorities do not have the ability to choose the amount of educational services they wish to purchase. In such cases, various desegregation policies for schools which significantly broaden the choice of schools could provide a substitute for choice through residential location, a choice which is often limited for minorities.

The importance of school choice is exemplified in the Boston METCO experience. Over 80 percent of participating black students reported that getting a better education was a very important factor in their participation, but almost 75 percent would prefer attending an equal quality school in their community.[19] And, in fact, participation does seem to have advantages to highly motivated, upwardly mobile blacks since they appear to be able to enter college more readily and to go to better schools after METCO participation. (On the other hand, the achievement of these students in suburban schools seems unaffected by the program.) The restriction of choice—while arising from aspects of society largely outside of the schools—must nevertheless be considered within school policies.

Community Control of Schools

The final policy proposal which relates directly to this study is community control of schools.[20] On the "educational" side this looks much like a compensatory plan. The real difference lies on the "political" side where there would exist a different structure of financial and management relationships. This plan calls for schools to be controlled by smaller communities than entire cities and would allow the development of faculties and curricula tailored to meet the particular needs of given groups found in different parts of the city. Within the context of the production functions estimated, it is difficult to distinguish between this proposal and compensatory programs with one exception: This plan may make the hiring of certain "community specific" school inputs politically feasible where it wouldn't otherwise be the case.

Take, for example, the case of Mexican-Americans analyzed here, where neither school inputs nor racial-social composition of the class appeared to matter. For this population existing technologies in the given school system do not seem to have much effect [f,21] Since blacks seem slightly more sensitive to

[f]This statement must be qualified. There are no differential effects among teachers. This does not say that the school system on average is doing worse or better than other school systems. The students progress at about one-half the average national rate of progression. Whether this is good or bad relative to what other school systems are doing for Mexican-Americans requires analysis of more than one school system. In absolute terms, the performance of one-half the average rate must be considered bad.

quality teachers than whites, this finding for Mexican-Americans does not appear to be a simple minority problem. The largest possibility seems to be the English language deficiency which often plagues this population in an English-speaking school. Therefore, the concept of community control might have more appeal here. If special needs of the population, say language, are not guaranteed by the central school administration, the case for community control appears clearer.

Restructuring Options

The previous set of options to change the distribution of education is certainly not complete. The unifying thread of the previous three policies is that they fall basically within the structure of the current system, but there is another set of proposals—largely untested—which calls for restructuring the public school system in an effort to make it more responsive to efficiency and distribution ideas. The two leading proposals for restructuring of public school incentives are educational vouchers and performance contracting.

Educational vouchers would provide parents with a tuition check which could be used at any certified school and, thus, would allow parents the opportunity to judge which school best met the needs of their children.[22] Schools would have an incentive to provide education efficiently, and, through competition among schools, the school system would presumably become more responsive to the desires of the community. The value of the vouchers could also be set in a compensatory manner to provide extra funding for the education of disadvantaged students. While experiments with vouchers have been proposed, none has been done to date.

Performance contracting provides for the hiring of private companies by public schools systems. These firms would supply schools with educational services, generally for remedial education in specific subject areas. The ultimate payment to the firms is linked to the achievement gains of individual students. While such an incentive scheme is appealing, the initial experiments with them, sponsored by the Office of Economic Opportunity, showed discouragingly small accomplishments by the contracting firms.[23]

The key provision in both of these proposals is the restructuring of incentives for schools. Conceptually they both represent movements in the right direction— toward management of the school system in terms of the outcomes of schools rather than input characteristics. However, these plans cannot be adequately judged within the framework of this or similar production function studies since they represent school organizations which are not observed in estimating the models of the educational process. To the extent that systems operating under either system utilize existing technologies, the models can give some estimates of the potential for elevating achievements. However, one of the key assumptions of both proposals is that new technologies will be explored and utilized. If this happens, the estimated models will be poor predictors of the potential gains, although they should provide an indication of the lower bound for potential change.

A Synthesis

It is difficult to make any generalizations about the various policy tools which could be used to change the distribution of education by race and ethnic group. Many of the decisions call for data about local areas, but these data are often unavailable. Much of the decision process is also political, and therein lies a series of issues which are very difficult to address in any scientific manner. The political nature of the discussion is well illustrated by a series of public pronouncements during a three week period in March 1972: The first National Black Political Convention voted to condemn busing to achieve racial desegregation, the President of the United States asked Congress to restrict the federal court use of busing for desegregation, and the National Policy Conference on Education for Blacks heard speakers decry the dangers of school apartheid.[24] The issues addressed in these arenas certainly cannot be fully addressed in a study such as this.

Nevertheless, some general observations can be made, particularly about desegregation and compensatory programs. From the course of the public debate and from the analyses here and elsewhere, it is evident that there are no panaceas, no miracle solutions to eliminate educational disparities by race, ethnic group, or social class. But the difficulties of eliminating *all* of the observed achievement gaps does not mean that no improvement is possible within the public schools; neither does it imply that the partial gains currently possible are not appropriate. This study presents a rather sanguine view of the possibilities of realizing gains with compensatory programs and some restructuring of the current school system. It also sees gains that could come from various desegregation policies—particularly if they allow a shift in the types of school resources that minorities could expect. There are two points of potential conflict between compensatory and desegregation programs: Desegregation could make compensatory programs more difficult by dispersing the disadvantaged population, and desegregation could draw upon funds which otherwise would be available for compensatory programs. Once the possibilities are recognized, little more can be said in the abstract.

There is no universal prescription leading to massive changes in the distribution of achievement that comes from adding up the costs and benefits of alternative programs. It is possible to delineate one set of programs which presumably would be generally advantageous such as no-cost desegregation programs (redistricting, pairing of schools, rerouting existing busing, etc.). It is possible to set out a list of generally more dubious programs (large decreases in class size, massive cross-busing in a relatively homogeneous system, etc.). Finally, there also exist a series of programs which fall into a "grey" area where no general statement can be made in the absence of more data about both the locale and the program (community control, vouchers, and so forth). But the overall choice of programs and administrative mechanisms is more a function of local political realities than of the scientific evidence supporting them.

Two things are clear from looking at major policy options: (1) the worst fears (in terms of detrimental aspects of proposals) appear unfounded, and (2) the current state of affairs is undesirable. Given this, a call for no action is not persuasive.

Needed Information

Current educational practices form the basis for all production function studies of education. This is a very serious limitation since it seems mandatory that the educational system consider change in a number of directions. For example, the techniques used within the schools have been highly resistant to technological innovation, particularly technological innovation of the labor saving variety. The current reliance upon labor intensive teaching methods without doubt has very important implications for the future costs of education. Within the framework of this analysis it has not been possible to evaluate any possible corrective measures in this direction. Also, frequently the claim is made that the curricula, teaching methods, and so forth are ones which have been developed for middle-class whites, but ones not necessarily best suited for minorities.[g] Yet, no "minority technology" has been well evaluated here.

School systems and educational technologies in fact appear very homogeneous, in many ways not much different from the systems and technologies of ancient Rome. The previous discussion has pointed out the possibilities for change basically within the current educational technology and, in that context, tends to take a somewhat sanguine view of the prospects—or at least of the technologically feasible prospects. Nevertheless, the need for experimentation is overwhelming. We need to test new technologies, new organizational structures, and new ways of viewing schools in society. There has been some movement in this direction: experiments with incentive contracting and proposals for voucher demonstrations are notable examples, not to mention the many technological ventures such as computer aided instruction.[25] But these ventures seem to lack the commitment and momentum which seems warranted if there are going to be significant changes in education through changes in technology.

Inquiries into the educational process have also rested upon one major dimension of output, cognitive development. *Particularly in the discussion of integration of the schools, other dimensions of output under the heading of socialization are extremely important, maybe even dominant.* Even in terms of economic potential of the individual student, other dimensions such as attitude formation or work habits are significant, perhaps to the extent of being more important than cognitive development.[26] These other dimensions may be harder

---

[g]The validity of this assertion might be questioned, given the equal or slightly greater impact of teachers on blacks than on whites. On the other hand, the analysis in chapters 4 and 5 indicated that, everything else being equal, performance in central cities was lower than in suburbs; this may be a partial reflection of inappropriate technologies.

to measure, but it is important that we discover the interrelationships among different measures of educational output.

Along the lines of measuring educational output, a vital piece of information is how society values education. Yet there are also large gaps in our knowledge about this. There are two separate facets to the valuation of education. First, the positive aspect considers what is the value of education to society and how do we best measure education when looked upon as an input into society. This has been the source of considerable past inquiry and continues to be the subject of research by a number of people.[27] Second, some consideration might be given to the normative aspects of societal valuation of education, i.e., what *should* schools be doing and what *should* society reward? These questions, of course, are not easy ones and are not the type which lead to quick consensuses. They are, however, central to the operations of public schools within the United States.

Past innovations in schooling have often been introduced into the schools with little prior experimentation or analysis. And once introduced these programs have not been subjected to the rigorous evaluation that is needed to ascertain whether they should be continued. This "fad" approach to schooling is clearly inefficient, at least given historical success rates on new programs, but there have been few resources and little attention devoted to learning from past history or to planning for the future.

The aftermath of the publication of *Equality of Educational Opportunity* is instructive in this regard. That report raised a series of fundamental questions about the schooling system and, in so doing, sparked considerable discussion about information needs and types of analyses which should be undertaken. By 1972, six years after that report and $7 billion dollars in federal grants for compensatory education later, there is no follow-up study on the horizon. The conclusion does not need stating.

A Final Word

Management of the educational system is a difficult task. The many participants in the management process lack complete freedom of action. Particularly at the federal and state level, there are serious, often legislated, limits on the range of direct or even indirect involvement possible for specific programs, but even local administrators do not have a free hand because of the complex interactions of school administrations, school boards, teachers' organizations, constituencies, and, now, student bodies. Nevertheless, limits on the scope of politically possible actions within schools may not be the most important impediment to improvement of public schooling. A more important impediment appears to be lack of knowledge about what actions should be undertaken. There has been very little systematic analysis of the educational process even though analysis of the educational process is well recognized as a key element needed for improving the educational system. Without such analysis it is not possible to decide rationally among alternative programs within the schools.

The term "analysis" as used here should not be taken as connoting just multimillion dollar, global studies of the educational system (although, as sketched in the previous section, some of those seem warranted). Instead, the term "analysis" is meant to imply using available information in a way that is useful for decision making. And it is appropriate to end with a short discussion of analysis at the local school system level since the bulk of educational decisions are made there.

Major school systems across the country routinely collect and store enormous amounts of data about the educational process, but these data are seldom processed in a way that is helpful to decision making in the school systems. The central lesson to be learned from the single system analysis (chapter 3) was how existing data collected by most school systems could be tabulated to provide an evaluation tool to decision makers. The heavy investment by local schools in data processing equipment and management information systems has largely been directed at improving accounting within schools; too little effort has been directed at improving decision making about the educational process itself. Without excessive effort, local school systems could develop supplemental evaluation information to aid in hiring teachers and deciding among programs. The failure to develop adequate analysis, or evaluation, at each level—federal, state and local—is all too evident.

Appendix

Appendix: The OE Survey Data

The Office of Education data, labeled the *OE Survey* here, were collected to satisfy a congressional requirement of conducting a survey to ascertain the extent of discrimination in public schools.[a] These data formed the basis for *Equality of Educational Opportunity* and a number of other analyses. This appendix points out some of the major weaknesses of the data when used for analyzing the educational process. A more detailed discussion of the reliability of particular questionnaire items along with some hypotheses about the effects of errors on subsequent analyses can be found in work by Christopher S. Jencks, and the interested reader is referred to that for more depth about the data problems.[b]

A stratified probability sampling technique which called for the overrepresentation of blacks was used to choose public high schools to be included in the survey. Feeder schools for the chosen high schools were included on a probability basis depending on the percentage of students going to the selected secondary schools.[c] While the sample size was originally administratively set at 900,000 students, nonresponses reduced the usable sample to approximately 570,000 students. These students were divided among grades 1, 3, 6, 9, and 12. Students were given ability and achievement tests and completed a questionnaire concerning family background and attitudes. Additionally, for the 3,155 schools which the students attended, data were gathered from teachers, principals, and school system superintendents. Teachers completed a questionnaire including background, attitudes, and school factors, along with an optional verbal facility test. Principals and superintendents supplied information about their backgrounds and attitudes and about school facilities in their particular school or district.[d]

Several points about the data deserve emphasis. First, the sample size is not as large as it appears. The effective size (for most statistical analyses) is not 570,000 observations, but instead the number of schools. (For elementary schools this number is approximately 2,400.) This reduction in effective sample size is caused by failure to collect the relevant school data for individual

---

[a]Section 402 of the Civil Rights Act of 1964 stated:

The Commissioner [of Education] shall conduct a survey and make a report to the President and the Congress, within two years of the enactment of this title, concerning the lack of availability of equal educational opportunities for individuals by reason of race, color, religion, or national origin in public educational institutions at all levels in the United States, its territories and possessions, and the District of Columbia.

[b]Christopher S. Jencks, "The Quality of Data Collected by the *Equality of Educational Opportunity* Survey," *On Equality of Educational Opportunity*.

[c]A detailed discussion of the sampling procedures can be found in *EEO*, pp. 550-58.

[d]Complete questionnaires and samples of test items are found in *EEO*.

students. While this sample size is still large, it is reduced considerably if stratification is necessary (e.g., by race, region, and grade).

The survey itself is plagued by nonresponse and faulty response. This problem is prevalent at the school level.[e] However, in the study of the educational process the problem of missing schools is not as serious as the problem of nonresponse or faulty response to individual questionnaire items. Analysis of the raw data indicated that many items could not be used in the production function estimation because of the severity of the nonresponse problem. This was particularly true in the case of emotionally sensitive questions such as the principal's attitudes toward busing, neighborhood schools, and faculty integration.[f] Faulty response also adds uncertainty to many questionnaire items.[g] This problem is more difficult to document. However, some feel for the problem can be gained from analysis of numerical items such as number of students or teachers. (The vast majority of questions call for multiple choice response as opposed to furnishing a numerical answer.) Since these can be cross-checked with other parts of the survey, they give some indication of the severity of the problem. Over 10 percent of the principals in Northeastern metropolitan elementary schools recorded an obviously incorrect answer—often due to left-justifying answers and, thus, creating decimal point errors. Since these questions required numerical coding (as opposed to the normal multiple choice questions), the expectation of faulty responses is greatest for these questions. However, from a further check by comparing responses in schools with two principals, it is obvious that the problem is not restricted to these items.[h]

Nevertheless, for the modeling of the educational process, the most severe problem with the data sources arises from a basic weakness, or incompleteness, in the questionnaires. There are several distinct and important dimensions to the incompleteness. There are the lack of historical information, the error in measuring contemporaneous inputs, and the neglect of several important sets of inputs.

While the conceptual model indicated that the history of inputs into the

---

[e]Of those high schools originally picked for the sample, 59 percent could be included in the final sample; 74 percent of the feeder schools picked for those high schools responding were included. In terms of making inferences about the population, extreme care must be exercised. There are indications of systematic nonresponse as several large central cities in the North failed to respond. (The exact character of this type of nonresponse cannot be analyzed due to the anonymity requirements of the survey.)

[f]For example, the principal's questionnaire contained three questions about attitudes on racial mix of the faculty under different racial compositions of the students. In a sample of approximately 300 elementary schools in the Northeast, over one third of the principals failed to answer one or more of the questions.

[g]The *OE Survey* did include one small-scale reliability test for student answers. However, this did not seem sufficient, especially after looking at the data.

[h]The simple check of question responses in dual principal schools provided the basis for many qualitative judgments which went into the variable construction and basic modeling efforts in the present analysis. The subjective evaluation of the reliability of various questions is discussed in chapters 4 and 5.

process is important in determining current educational output, there is a definite lack of such information. This failure, arising from a neglect to include any questions about previous factors, impinges upon the measurement of all inputs. However, it is potentially more severe in the case of school inputs. School inputs have more of the characteristics of flows, and a cross-sectional glimpse of contemporaneous inputs does a relatively poorer job of measuring the stream of inputs (as opposed to cross-sectional measures of the family inputs into the educational process). This problem is particularly acute in later grades of school as high schools and even junior highs tend to draw students from quite heterogeneous feeder schools. Obviously, the size of historical errors of measurement increases over time.

Yet, even at measuring the contemporaneous values of inputs into the educational process, the *OE Survey* has its difficulties. The most crucial problem on these grounds is the failure to collect data on the school inputs relevant to the individual student. All school information comes from the principal or superintendent responses without regard for how the total available inputs are distributed to individuals. It is obvious that students attending the same school do not receive the same school inputs. The presence of science laboratories does not affect a student in a business course. Extracurricular activities are largely irrelevant to a lower-class person who must work after school. The list of differentiation in inputs is unending. The simple presence of a particular input does not imply that the factor enters the educational process of any given individual. Furthermore, there are some systematic components to such errors in the measurement of school inputs for the individual. Certainly the errors are very much dependent on the school organization. The error component of the school inputs can be enormous in the case of the comprehensive high school. Basically, the larger and more complex the school, the larger is the expected error in the measurement of school inputs for the individual. The errors will also be correlated with other inputs into the process such as social class since choice of curriculum and schools is correlated with social class. (To the extent that these errors are systematic, sizable errors will arise when statistical estimation is undertaken. When important, these are discussed in chapters 4-6.)

The final problem area with the questionnaires arises from a tendency to stop short of asking many logical and important questions. This is most evident in the case of school inputs; however, it does arise in the nonschool areas. The best description of this problem is a failure to gather qualitative information about the various inputs. There are many questions pertaining to presence of facilities or programs, but few pertaining to quality. For example, there is extremely little information on school organization; there is no information on the adequacy of facilities such as laboratories or even the overall plant. This lack of a quality dimension makes it extremely difficult to differentiate among schools in terms of many school inputs. (This is not serious in the single system analysis since these factors are relatively constant across schools.)

Nevertheless, the discussion of the problem areas with the data should not be construed as implying that the data are worthless. Quite clearly the data are not ideal. However, the survey does contain much valuable information. The *OE Survey* provides a large sample of consistent data which can be used to analyze many questions of current interest in education. The findings will necessarily be less conclusive than if an ideal set of data were available. Yet, by recognizing the sources of errors in the data it is possible to devise models of the educational process which minimize the problems.

Notes

Notes

Chapter 1
Topics in Public Education

1. The President's Commission on School Finance, *Schools, People and Money* (Washington, D.C.: Government Printing Office, 1972).

2. See John F. Kain, "The Distribution and Movement of Jobs and Industry," in James Q. Wilson (ed.), *The Metropolitan Enigma* (Cambridge: Harvard University Press, 1968), for an overview of the intrametropolitan area trends.

3. Dick Netzer, *The Economics of the Property Tax* (Washington, D.C.: The Brookings Institution, 1967), gives a thorough account of the changes in tax base in the central city.

4. James A. Maxwell, *Financing State and Local Governments* (Washington, D.C.: The Brookings Institution, 1965), shows that a majority of states have local debt limits requiring referendum votes for increased expenditures (pp. 194-99).

5. George Break suggests several alternative formulas for providing intergovernmental grants. However, they all seem to neglect many of the crucial issues of the efficiency problem as found in practice. Among other things, these analyses implicitly assume that local governments know the production function available. That is exactly what this study is attempting to uncover. See *Intergovernmental Fiscal Relations in the United States* (Washington, D.C.: The Brookings Institution, 1967).

6. U.S. Bureau of the Census, *Statistical Abstract of the United States, 1971.* (Washington, D.C.: Government Printing Office, 1971).

7. These figures result from a nationwide survey of public schools by the Office of Education in 1965. These data are described in detail in chapter 4, since they are used in the subsequent analysis. The tabulations are found in James S. Coleman et al., *Equality of Educational Opportunity* (Washington, D.C.: Government Printing Office, 1966), subsequently referred to as *EEO*.

8. Otherwise known as the Kerner Commission Report. (Otto Kerner et al.), *Report of the National Advisory Commission on Civil Disorders* (Washington, D.C.: Government Printing Office, 1968).

Chapter 2
A Conceptual Model of the Educational Process

1. *Equality of Educational Opportunity*, frequently called the *Coleman Report* after its principal author, was not the first analysis of the educational

process but probably remains the most influential. Other major research efforts in this area are included in the bibliography at the end of this book and are critiqued and summarized in a number of places. See, for example, Samuel Bowles, "Toward An Educational Production Function," in W. Lee Hansen (ed.) *Education, Income, and Human Capital* (New York: National Bureau of Economic Research, 1970) or James W. Guthrie et al., *Schools and Inequality* (Cambridge: MIT Press, 1971).

2. The notions behind the production function can be traced back to David Ricardo when he stated the law of diminishing returns in the early 1800s. However, it was the mathematical formulation of the production function by Augustin Cournot and Leon Walras in the mid-1800s which demonstrated its theoretical usefulness. A modern, mathematical treatment of production functions is found in James H. Henderson and Richard E. Quandt, *Microeconomic Theory* (New York: McGraw-Hill Book Co., 1958).

3. This is an oversimplification; prices can be quite different to ascertain, particularly in education. Cf. Henry Levin, "Recruiting Teachers for Large City Schools" (mimeo).

4. For a discussion of learning theories, see Ernest B. Hilgard, *Theories of Learning*, 2nd ed. (New York: Appleton-Century-Croft, Inc., 1965). Other work on the process itself is reviewed in Harvey A. Averch, et al., *How Effective is Schooling?*, R-956-PCSF/RC (Santa Monica: The RAND Corp., 1972).

5. Complete freedom of choice of time horizons is not always available to analysts because of data constraints. Cross-sectional data usually imply looking at the whole range of schooling because $A_{it}*$ is missing. One example of an attempt at a limited production time is Jesse Burkhead, *Input and Output in Large-City High School* (Syracuse: Syracuse University Press, 1967). However, as indicated in his work, when the time horizon gets too small, our measurement talents are not developed well enough to pick up changes in achievement.

6. An example of the traditional list of goals can be found in George R. Cressman and Harold W. Benda, *Public Education in America*, 3rd ed. (New York: Appleton-Century-Crofts, 1966), pp. 193-207. This section also illustrates the difficulties in attempting to develop precise definition. "The educated person should . . . "

7. One issue often introduced at this point is the view that schools primarily relate to job and income through the selection process. Completing a given level of schooling implies both some minimal ability level and a mixture of tenacity, self-discipline, and "proper" attitudes. In this framework, schools are looked at mostly as a screening device; any specific, job-related skills are provided by the firm. This hypothesis has been developed recently by Herbert Gintis, "Education, Technology, and the Characteristics of Worker Productivity," *American Economic Review*, May 1971. However, this hypothesis seems less relevant to the study of schools as long as one adequately considers the quantity of schooling (number of years) and as long as within given quantity groups higher

specific skills relate to better jobs. If this holds, the selection hypothesis pertains only to the mechanism of rewarding the skill component of education and, thus, does not affect the explicit consideration of skill development in the schools. Support of the relationship between achievement and income is found in W. Lee Hansen, Burton A. Weisbrod, and William J. Scanlon, "Schooling and Earnings of Low Achievers," *American Economic Review*, June 1970; Burton A. Weisbrod and Peter Karpoff, "Monetary Returns to College Education, Student Ability, and College Quality," *The Review of Economics and Statistics*, November 1968, pp. 491-97; Randall D. Weiss, "The Effects of Education on the Earnings of Blacks and Whites," *Review of Economics and Statistics*, Feb. 1970; Eric A. Hanushek, "Regional Differences in the Structure of Earnings," Discussion Paper No. 66, Program on Regional and Urban Economics, Harvard University, 1971; and Zvi Griliches and William Mason, "Education, Income, and Ability," Discussion Paper No. 207, Harvard Institute of Economic Research, 1971.

This differs in outlook from the basic framework of Talcott Parsons in "The School Class as a Social System," *Harvard Educational Review*, Fall 1959, where he divides the functions of schools into selection and socialization. His socialization includes both developing skills and preparing the child to use them in society.

8. Throughout this discussion, the terms "ability" and "achievement" are used interchangeably. In a strictly conceptual formulation it is possible to differentiate between the two with ability applying to "potential" and achievement apply to "attainment." However, it is generally conceded that this formal distinction is not really operationally useful since one cannot measure some unchanging item called ability or potential. This is discussed thoroughly in Benjamin S. Bloom, *Stability and Change in Human Characteristics* (New York: John Wiley and Sons, Inc., 1964), and J. McV. Hunt, *Intelligence and Experience* (New York: The Ronald Press Co., 1961). The major difference between ability tests and achievement tests is the scope of the test (ability being broader). Both will vary with differences in environment. Thus, the semantical distinction is not made in this book. One necessary postscript, however, is mention of the controversy stirred up by Arthur R. Jensen, "How Much Can We Boost IQ and Scholastic Achievement," *Harvard Educational Review*, Winter 1968, where he argues from empirical studies that environment doesn't play a large part in determining IQ test scores. This controversy, continued in the *Harvard Educational Review* of Spring 1969, goes far beyond the scope of this discussion and, therefore, is only noted in passing.

9. There is a related issue on scale of measurement for achievement test scores which should be mentioned, although it will not be resolved here. Absolute scores, say on an achievement test, can introduce some confusion. It is true that a higher score is better. Yet, how much better? Is a score of fifty twice as good as a score of twenty-five or is it only one and a half times as good? Test

scores give an ordinal measure of achievement. The numerical scale is basically as good as an order-preserving transformation of itself. Related to this is the determination of the scale of the test in terms of difficulty of various questions. It might be easier to gain five points on a test at the low end (for example, going from zero to five points) than at the upper end. The extreme example of this is a ceiling on the test where it is possible to obtain a perfect score. The point is simple; an incremental gain in output (measured by standardized tests) may have different meanings over different ranges of the test. One attempt to add a degree of cardinality to the measure is the transformation into grade level equivalents. However, this is only a partial solution: (1) the variance of the population must remain constant, and (2) it is still not possible to say sixth grade achievement is twice as good as third grade achievement.

A more detailed discussion of scales of measurement and transformations of achievement test scores is found in James S. Coleman and Nancy L. Karweit, *Measures of School Performance*, R-488-RC (Santa Monica: The RAND Corp., 1970).

10. Examples of the emphasis on quantity are found in the extensive work on economic growth. See E.F. Denison, "Measuring the Contribution of Education (and the Residual) to Economic Growth," in *The Residual Factor and Economic Growth* (Paris: OECD, 1964).

11. Using twelfth grade whites in the urban Northeast as the norm, twelfth grade blacks in the rural South are 5.1 grade levels behind in verbal ability. See *EEO*, Table 3.121.1, which is repeated here in Table 1-1.

12. One example of this approach is found in Weiss, "The Effect of Education."

13. For more on quantity, see Weisbrod, "Preventing High School Dropouts" in Robert Dorfman (ed.), *Measuring Benefits of Government Investment* (Washington, D.C.: Brookings Institution, 1965).

14. See Hansen, Weisbrod, and Scanlon, "Determinants of Earnings." This evidence applies to a very select sample, men who failed Armed Forces Qualifying Tests. Nevertheless, the argument is reasonable a priori. The primary problem is finding a good measure of quality which relates to the additional experiences of additional years of schooling. There is also mixed evidence on this score. Cf. Hanushek, "Regional Differences" and Griliches and Mason, "Education, Income, and Ability."

15. See note 7 above.

16. There exists a wide range of literature pertaining to socialization. For a collection of more traditional articles on socialization, see "Socialization and Schools," *Harvard Educational Review*, Reprint Series No. 1, 1968. This includes articles by James S. Coleman, Robert Dreeben, Alex Inkeles, and Talcott Parsons. A wide range of popular books also exist. For example, Jonathan Kozol, *Death at an Early Age* (Boston: Houghton-Mifflin, 1968); Charles E. Silberman, *Crisis in the Classroom* (New York: Random House,

1970); and Ivan Illich, *Deschooling Society* (New York: Harper and Row, 1971). Finally, there have been some empirical studies. The relationship between socialization and incomes or occupational status has received little attention in the past. A formulation of the possible mechanism for such relationships and crude tests of the significance of any relationships can be found in Herbert Gintis, "Education, Technology and the Characteristics of Worker Productivity."

17. The formal solution, presented in Henderson and Quandt, *Microeconomic Theory*, pp. 67-75, integrates the relative prices of jointly produced outputs into the simple, one output decision rule. Such prices are difficult to find within education, and, thus, the general rule couldn't be applied even with knowledge of the complete production function. There are nevertheless circumstances which ameliorate the difficulties encountered in the general case.

It may be plausible to assume that the outputs are produced in fixed proportions. Given some overall conception of what should result from schooling, teachers might, through set curricula or voluntarily, aim for the same mix of output. This seems particularly reasonable within a given curriculum such as college preparatory in high school or within an elementary school. In this case, the simple decision rule applies because the output mix problem has been solved.

Another simple case assumes that it is possible to develop some index which relates the various outputs of the production process. Such a weighting scheme would act in the same way that prices act in the market situation. This is a very real possibility since school administrators tend to do this implicitly with regularity.

If all of the inputs which come under governmental control and thus hired by the decision maker bear the same relationship to each of the individual outputs, i.e., have proportional marginal products with each of the outputs, it is again possible to use the simple rule for hiring inputs as applied to any one of the outputs. In other words, efficiency in any direction of output is equivalent to efficiency in all directions in this special case. This case exists when schools have the same relative impact in any direction in which energy is applied. (To be correct the rule requires a further stringent assumption that the marginal product of an input in any direction depends on the total usage of that input, not just the usage directly aimed at a given output).

18. This is thoroughly discussed in Glenn Cain and Harold Watts, "Problems in Making Policy Inferences from the Coleman Report," *American Sociological Review*, April 1970.

19. A thorough treatment of these issues can be found in Frank S. Levy, *Northern Schools and Civil Rights* (Chicago: Markham Publishing Co., 1971). The effects of composition are also central to many studies. See, for example, Alan B. Wilson, "Educational Consequences of Segregation in a California Community," *Racial Isolation in the Public Schools, Appendices* (Washington, D.C.: GPO, 1967).

20. See note 8, above.

21. See, for example, J. Cravioto and E.R. De Licardie, "The Long-Term Consequences of Protein-Calorie Malnutrition," *Nutrition Reviews* 29 5 (May 1971).

22. The fact that given students can be excluded from certain school services means that schools are not pure public goods according to traditional economic theory. It has implications when one considers the level of investment in education and the distribution of educational services. The notion of excluded individuals from certain services has even been carried into the classroom, e.g., David S. Mundel, "Modeling the Classroom" (mimeo, 1969).

Chapter 3
Single System, Individual Student Analysis

1. For example, Eric Hanushek and John Kain, "On the Value of *Equality of Educational Opportunity* as a Guide to Public Policy," in Frederick Mosteller and Daniel P. Moynihan (eds.) *On Equality of Educational Opportunity* (New York: Random House, 1972).

2. Edgar F. Borgatta and Raymond J. Corsini, *Quick Word Test: Level 2* (New York: Harcourt, Brace and World, Inc., 1964). This test appears to be superior to the test in *Equality of Educational Opportunity* as it appears to give better discrimination among teachers. One complaint voiced about the *EEO* test is that it was too easy.

The complete survey of teachers can be found in Eric Hanushek, *The Value of Teachers in Teaching* RM-6362-CC/RC (Santa Monica: The RAND Corp., 1970), Appendix A.

3. The extent of pupil mobility in elementary and secondary schools is described in A. Stafford Metz, "Pupil Mobility in Public Elementary and Secondary Schools during the 1968-69 School Year," National Center for Educational Statistics (Washington, D.C.: Government Printing Office, 1971).

4. Silberman explains this in terms of the noncognitive goals which he sees in schools: "This encouragement of docility may explain why girls tend to be more successful in school than boys: passivity and docility are more in keeping with the behavior the culture expects of girls outside of school than the behavior it expects of boys." Charles E. Silberman, *Crisis in the Classroom* (New York: Random House, 1970), pp. 152-53.

5. See, for example, *EEO*, chapter 3.

6. U.S., Congress, Senate, *Equal Educational Opportunity*, Part 1A, 91st Cong., 2nd Session, 1970, p. 32.

7. Mary Ellen Leary, "Are Children Who Are Tested in an Alien Language Mentally Retarded?" *The New Republic*, May 30, 1970.

8. See Henry M. Levin (ed.), *Community Control of Schools* (Washington, D.C.: The Brookings Institution, 1969).

Chapter 4
Multisystem Analysis–White Education

1. See Benjamin S. Bloom, *Stability and Change of Human Characteristics* (New York: John Wiley and Sons, Inc., 1964), for a synopsis of longitudinal studies depicting changes in ability as commonly measured. Also, Hunt, *Intelligence and Experience*, presents similar evidence along with a discussion of fixed versus interactive theories of intelligence.

2. Cf. *EEO*, p. 293.

3. *Equality of Educational Opportunity* and *Racial Isolation in the Public Schools* both base their findings exclusively on the relationships involving verbal ability. (The *EEO* presents a very unconvincing argument for doing this based on relative amounts of variance in the test scores found between schools and an even weaker argument making intergrade variance comparisons.) However, in addition to these published works, all re-analysis is, to my knowledge, concentrating on verbal achievement.

4. Kiesling, "Efficiency of School Districts," notes very different expenditure and size characteristics for rural schools. His regression analyses of district achievement also indicates quite different production relationships. See especially Chapter 3.

5. These are 1960 figures for the entire population, not just school age children. U.S. Bureau of the Census. *U.S. Census of Population: 1960. General Social and Economic Characteristics, United States Summary*. Final Report PC(1)-1C. (Washington, D.C.: U.S. Government Printing Office, 1962), pp. 1-250.

6. U.S. Commission on Civil Rights, *Racial Isolation in the Public Schools* (Washington, D.C.: Government Printing Office, 1967).

7. An example of experiments showing different dimensions is found in Susan S. Stodolsky and Gerald Lesser, "Learning Patterns in the Disadvantaged," *Harvard Educational Review* 37 (Fall 1967): 547-93. Also see the summary of different investigations in Bloom, *Stability*.

8. The study of environmental influences on achievement has been the subject of an untold number of studies of man and animal. The reactions of white mice and the abilities of separated twins have confirmed the effect of favorable environment on raising educational levels. The important environmental factors are additionally highly correlated with socioeconomic status. Surveys of important pieces of research in this area are found in Bloom, *Stability*, and Hunt, *Intelligence and Experience*.

9. U.S. Bureau of the Census, *U.S. Census of Housing, 1960. Volume I, States and Small Areas. Part I: United States Summary* (Washington, D.C.: U.S. Government Printing Office, 1963), pp. 1-44. The figures apply to all SMSAs. The suburban ring includes all of the SMSA outside of the central city.

10. A reliability test of the *OE Survey* occupation question by J. David

Colfax and Irving Allen indicated that among their sample of sixth graders, over 50 percent either failed to respond or responded incorrectly. See "Pre-Coded versus Open-Ended Items and Children's Reports of Father's Occupation," *Sociology of Education* 40 (Winter 1967): 96-98. Additionally, the question is divided in such a manner that it is not possible to sort occupations along traditional white collar and blue collar lines.

11. Cf. Bloom, *Stability*, pp. 214-16.

12. Cf. J. Johnston, *Econometric Methods* (New York: McGraw-Hill Book Co., 1963), pp. 148-50.

13. Doubts about the lasting effects of intensive preschool were introduced by the Westinghouse Learning Corp., "The Impact of Head Start," June 1969.

14. See, for example, the recommendations of the McElroy Commission, *Schools, People, and Money.*

15. The elasticity for teacher verbal ability goes from .125 to .119; for experience from .019 to .022; and for nonwhite teachers from $-.023$ to $-.025$. Thus, for the interesting section of the educational production function, there is little difference in the parameter estimates for the structural equation and the reduced form equation.

Alternative estimates of simultaneous equation estimates can be found in Henry Levin, "A New Model of School Effectiveness," in U.S. Office of Education, *Do Teachers Make A Difference?* (Washington, D.C.: Government Printing Office, 1969).

16. A parameter estimate is biased when the expected value of the estimate does not equal the true value. It is inconsistent if the estimate does not converge on the true value in the probability limit. Discussion of a simultaneous model can be found in Levin, "A New Model of School Effectiveness."

17. The essential feature is that inconsistency is not a discrete process but a continuous process. It is sometimes desirable to trade some inconsistency for the desirable properties of least squares (e.g., minimum variance). Cf. Franklin M. Fisher, "On the Cost of Approximate Specification in Simultaneous Equation Estimation," *Econometrica* 29 (April 1961): 139-70.

18. A discussion of the explicit shortcomings of *EEO* is found in Hanushek and Kain, "On the Value of *Equality of Educational Opportunity* As a Guide to Public Policy" and in Bowles and Levin, "The Determinants of Scholastic Achievement—An Appraisal of Some Recent Evidence."

19. While unidirectional causality from teacher quality to student achievement is always assumed in this study, it should be noted that there are hypotheses to the contrary. Emil J. Haller in "Pupil Influence in Teacher Socialization: A Socio-Linguistic Study," *Sociology of Education*, Fall 1967, pp. 316-33, suggests that causality might run in the opposite direction. His tests were unconvincing, and this author has no qualms about assuming unidirectional causality.

20. Two questions provide information on teachers' choice of schools:

29. How did you happen to be assigned to this particular school rather than some other school in this district?

(A) I asked to work in this school

(B) I was placed in this school

38. If you could choose, would you be a faculty member in some other school rather than this one?

(A) Yes

(B) Maybe

(C) No

EEO, pp. 678-79.

21. *EEO*, Chapter IV, and James A. Davis, *Undergraduate Career Decisions* (Chicago: Aldine Publishing Co., 1965).

22. Cf. J. Johnston, *Econometric Methods*, pp. 148-50.

23. Something similar to this seems to be suggested by Bloom, who traces out the longitudinal pattern of achievement growth and concludes the following about the first few years of schooling: "These are the years in which general learning patterns develop most rapidly, and failure to develop appropriate achievement and learning in these years is likely to lead to continued failure throughout the remainder of the individual's school career." Bloom, *Stability*, p. 127.

24. This particular variable actually provides a poor test of two competing hypotheses. Mel Ravitz advocates more male teachers for the disadvantaged because of the matriarchal structure of the family. See "The Role of the School in the Urban Setting," in A. Harry Passow (ed.) *Education in Depressed Areas* (New York: Teachers College Press of Teachers College, Columbia University, 1963). This would suggest that more male teachers should have a positive relationship with achievement. On the other hand, since male teachers are generally of lower quality (see Davis, *Undergraduate Career Decisions*), this variable could be interpreted as another teacher quality measure with an expected negative relationship. This conflicting aspect could be responsible for the insignificant effect on achievement.

25. This measure is used extensively by Kiesling, "Efficiency of School Districts." It is also a standard means of comparing schools as in the Civil Rights Commission report, *Racial Isolation*.

26. The *OE Survey* contains district-wide expenditure data. These were used by in *EEO* to construct a per pupil expenditure figure for school districts. However, large differences in expenditures are known to exist within systems. These differences are systematic both by the grade level of the school (high school, junior high, elementary) and by social class and race. (Cf. Katzman, *The Political Economy of Urban Schools* and Patricia Cayo Sexton, *Education and Income* (New York: The Viking Press, 1961). These systematic errors make the district figure worthless for our purposes.

27. Levin gives some insight into this. He shows differences between teacher

costs in different regions which are applicable to this study. Both his Eastmet and Midmet are metropolitan areas which fall within the sample for this study. Additionally, he shows that there are cost differences between teachers in the central city and the ring and differences *within* the same city arising from difficult schools. See Levin, "Recruiting Teachers for Large City Schools" (unpublished manuscript, The Brookings Institution, 1968), especially chapters VI and VII.

28. These figures apply to 1963-64 elementary and secondary school operations. For elementary schools alone, the figures would be larger. Kenneth A. Simon and W. Vance Grant, *Digest of Educational Statistics: 1967 Edition* (Washington, D.C.: Government Printing Office, 1967), p. 59.

29. James Coleman makes this clear in an article discussing the findings in *Equality of Educational Opportunity.* In part he states:

Even the school-to-school variation in achievement, though relatively small, is itself almost wholly due to the social environment provided by the school; the educational backgrounds and aspirations of other students in the school, and the educational backgrounds and attainments of the teachers in the school. *Per pupil expenditure, books in the library, and a host of other facilities and curricular measures show virtually no relation to achievement if the "social" environment school—the educational backgrounds of other students and teachers—is held constant.*

James S. Coleman, "Equal Schools or Equal Students," *Public Interest*, Fall 1966, p. 73.

Chapter 5
Multisystem Analysis—Black Education

1. Joseph Alsop, "No More Nonsense About Ghetto Education," *The New Republic*, July 22, 1967, p. 18.

2. The extent of ghettoization of cities is described in Karl E. Taeuber and Alma F. Taeuber, *Negroes in Cities* (Chicago: Aldine Publishing Co., 1965). With neighborhood schools and concentrations of blacks in ghettoes, the percentage of blacks will cluster at the two extremes.

3. The evidence on input differences is mostly fragmentary, but it is consistent across studies. There are many studies which show differences in inputs between central cities and suburbs, e.g., the per pupil expenditure figures presented in the Civil Rights Commission Report, *Racial Isolation in the Public Schools.* The central city-suburb distinction is, in many ways, a black-white distinction. Also, there is some evidence of systematic differences in school inputs by race within the same city, e.g., Patricia Cayo Sexton, "City Schools," *The Annals of the American Academy of Political and Social Science*, 352 (March 1964): 95-106; Martin Katzman, *The Political Economy of Urban Schools;* and *A Report by the Governor's Commission on the LA Riots:*

Violence in the City—An End or a Beginning?, December 1965, pp. 49-61. There is considerable controversy over the extent of discrimination in school inputs by race. Unfortunately, *Equality of Educational Opportunity* did not provide the answers to these distribution questions. There are indications that the Title I money that goes to schools with disadvantaged children is changing these patterns of input distribution. Nonetheless, these funds did not exist for the children in this study.

4. The importance of migration is well documented in a number of sources. See John Kain and Joseph Persky, "The North's Stake in Southern Rural Poverty," in John Kain and John Meyer (eds.), *Essays in Regional Economics* (Cambridge: Harvard University Press, 1971); Karl E. Taeuber and Alma F. Taeuber, *Negroes in Cities*, Chapter 6; and Eva Mueller and William Ladd, "Negro-White Differences in Geographic Mobility," in Louis A. Ferman, Joyce L. Kornbluh, and J.A. Miller (eds.), *Negroes and Jobs* (Ann Arbor: University of Michigan Press, 1968).

5. These figures are tabulated in Kain and Persky, "The North's Stake in Southern Rural Poverty," from data in the One in a Thousand sample of the 1960 Census of Population.

6. In the realm of education these differences are well documented in *Equality of Educational Opportunity*. Regional differences coincide with much larger quality differentials for blacks than whites, as is vividly shown in educational output by race and region, such as the statistics reproduced in table 1-2 of this book.

7. Daniel Patrick Moynihan, *The Negro Family: The Case for National Action* (Office of Policy Planning and Research, United States Department of Labor, March, 1965), p. 30.

8. For example, discussions of family structure and the matriarchal system are found in Thomas F. Pettigrew, *A Profile of the Negro American* (Princeton, N.J.: D. Van Nostrand, Inc., 1964); Harold L. Shepard and Herbert D. Striner, "Family Structure and Employment Problems" in *Negroes and Jobs*, pp. 174-87; and Mel Ravitz, "The Role of the School in the Urban Setting."

9. U.S. Bureau of Census. *Census of the Population, 1960, Nonwhite Population by Race*, PC(2)-1c (Washington, D.C.: U.S. Government Printing Office, 1963), pp. 9-10.

10. *Racial Isolation*, p. 104, quoted from the testimony of Dr. Charles Pinderhughes at the Boston Hearings of the Civil Rights Commission.

Chapter 6
Race and Public Education

1. "Text of the President's Statement Explaining His Policy on School Desegregation," In U.S. Senate, *Equal Educational Opportunity*, Part 1A, 1970, p. 4.

2. See Hanushek and Kain, "On the Value of *Equality of Educational Opportunity*," for a discussion of some of the data shortcomings. Some intensive analysis into the *OE Survey* has indicated strong and systematic differences in educational inputs by income and race. This is presented in John Owen, "The Distribution of Educational Resources in Large American Cities," *Journal of Human Resources*, Winter 1972.

3. The most persuasive case for changing the method of financing schools is found in John E. Coons, Wm. Clune, and Stephen Sugarman, *Private Wealth and Public Education* (Cambridge: Belknap Press, 1971). This book also reviews current financing plans.

4. The two most notable policy recommendations along these lines appear in the President's Commission on School Finance, *Schools, People, and Money* (The McElroy Commission Report) and in the *Report of the New York State Commission on the Quality, Cost and Financing of Elementary and Secondary Education* (The Fleischmann Commission Report). The actual proposals differ somewhat, but the concepts are very similar between them.

5. These figures apply to the 1965-55 school year (except for Cleveland which apply to 1962-63). *Racial Isolation*, pp. 4-5. A more complete tabulation of the extent of segregation is found in the *Racial Isolation*, Vol. II (Appendices), pp. 2-19 and in *Statistical Abstract of the United States, 1971*. p. 117.

6. *EEO*, pp. 289-90.

7. *Racial Isolation*, Vol. II. (Appendices), pp. 63 and 65. It is important, however, to recognize that these observations about racial composition effects on attitudes are arrived at through very incomplete attitude models. Thus, they are subject to many of the criticisms below.

8. These impressions arise from a variety of sources. Irwin Katz reviews evidence relating to behavioral pressures on blacks when they are mixed with whites. See "Review of Evidence Relating to Effects of Desegregation on the Performance of Negroes," *American Psychologist*, 19 (1964): 381-99. Also, Thomas F. Pettigrew, *A Profile of the Negro American* Princeton: D. Van Nostrand Company, Inc., 1964), especially Chapter 2, discusses the various attitudes of blacks to segregation in general and their relations with whites. The *Kerner Commission Report*, pp. 174-78, presents evidence on black attitudes in the Newark and Detroit ghettoes after the riots. A thorough review of the psychological development of the segregated black is found in David P. Ausabel and Pearl Ausabel, "Ego Development Among Segregated Negro Children," in Passow (ed.), *Education in Depressed Areas*, pp. 109-41.

9. From Group for the Advancement of Psychiatry, *Psychiatric Aspects of School Desegregation* (New York: GAP, 1957), p. 10, as quoted in Katz, "Desegregation," p. 387.

10. Statement by Calvin Brooke at the Cleveland Hearings of the Civil Rights Commission, as quoted in *Racial Isolation*, p. 104.

11. In a summary of black job market studies, Melvin Lurie and Elton

Rayack point out that well over half of all jobs are found by informal search procedures (friends, relatives, etc.). "Racial Differences in Migration and Job Search: A Case Study," *The Southern Economic Journal*, July 1966.

12. See U.S. Senate, *Equal Educational Opportunity*, Part 1A, p. 74.

13. *Kerner Commission Report*, p. 438. The concluding sentence was part of the testimony of Dr. Dan W. Dodson.

14. Many studies with racial separations and integrations are reviewed in Martha Carithers, "School Desegregation and Racial Cleavage, 1954-1970; A Review of the Literature," *Journal of Social Issues* 26, 4. Here one finds that the expectations for desegregation are not uniformly favorable, but instead depend on the particular setting, the age of the individual, the sex of the individual, and so forth.

15. While several re-analyses of *OE Survey* data have included racial composition of schools as one facet of the discussion, the re-analyses of David K. Cohen, Thomas F. Pettigrew, and Robert T. Reilly is illustrative as its sole interest is racial composition. See "Race and the Outcomes of Schooling," *On Equality of Educational Opportunity*.

16. The clearest exposition of the different aspects, especially social class and racial composition, can be found in *Racial Isolation*. A discussion of various remedies can be found in *Racial Isolation*, chapter 4, and in the *Kerner Commission Report*, p. 424-56.

17. *Racial Isolation*, p. 114.

18. The first test of the racial composition hypothesis is found on page 90 of *Racial Isolation*. This appears to be the basic test of the racial composition hypothesis. The plethora of alternative models makes precision in documenting the analysis difficult.

19. *Racial Isolation* uses the percentage white classmates last year (divided into the ranges none, less than half, about half, more than half). This represents a slightly different factor to the extent that other minorities are present and present racial composition differs from that last year.

20. As mentioned previously, it is difficult to discover much more than direction of movement from the contingency table analysis. It was hoped that through aggregating the contingency tables over individuals some rough comparisons of achievement differences between the two extremes could be made, i.e., comparisons of achievement levels in few black and all black schools of a given social class. However, there is a units problem in relating the two analyses as *Racial Isolation* uses "scale scores" and the production function estimates here are based on raw test scores. The scale scores are two steps removed from the raw scores. First, the raw scores were converted to a national mean equal to 50 with a standard deviation of 10. (Raw scores in the sixth grade range from 0 to 50.) The scale scores represent conversions of these standardized scores according to the following formulas found on p. 36 of *Racial Isolation:*

12th grade stnd. score = (scale score − 220) x .6254 + 10.2571

9th grade stnd. score = (scale score − 220) x .6539 + 16.8845

There are two problems. First, no handy formula was given for the sixth grade and, thus, direct comparisons with the sixth grade contingency tables are not possible. (Extrapolation from the two formulas seemed hazardous.) Second, reaching the standardized scores from the raw scores requires a nonlinear transformation which was unknown. Consequently, even rough comparisons with ninth or twelfth grade were not possible.

21. These findings are not qualitatively different from those in Cohen, Pettigrew, and Riley, "Race and Outcomes of Schooling." They tend to argue, however, that much of the observed low effect of different racial compositions on black achievement is due to errors in measurement of the composition variable, rather than in the form of the output variable. Their arguments about the racial composition variable—that percentage black does not accurately portray school atmosphere, hostility, etc.—are undoubtedly important but, at the same time, seem secondary to the issue of what question is the appropriate one to ask.

22. *Racial Isolation*, p. 160, makes passing reference to evidence that whites are not hurt by integration. They do not seriously analyze this question.

23. This inability to test peer effects relates to the inappropriateness of the data for modeling individual education. Peer effects have been widely discussed recently. However, most of this discussion arises from "findings" of the *EEO*, which used the *OE Survey* data for individual analysis.

24. Earl Raab (ed.), *American Race Relations Today* (Garden City, N.Y.: Anchor Books, Doubleday and Company, Inc., 1962), p. 81.

Chapter 7
Summary and Beyond

1. Importance can be measured in a number of ways. Several past studies, for example *Equality of Educational Opportunity*, have concentrated on the proportion of achievement variance which can be explained by variations in family inputs. By this criterion, families are quite important. However, this criterion is ambiguous in this situation and is not the most meaningful measure of importance. See Hanushek and Kain, "On the Value of *Equality of Educational Opportunity*," or G.G. Cain and H.W. Watts, "Problems of Making Policy Inferences." Alternatively, importance can be measured by size of the regression coefficient. On this ground, families still assume importance. Finally, importance could, as suggested by Cain and Watts, be determined by regression coefficients normalized by price of changing an input. In this case, families no longer seem "important."

2. Examples of erroneous interpretations of estimated educational models are not difficult to find. For example, a recent statement on education by the

Department of Health, Education and Welfare said, "A major underlying assumption of the President's welfare reform initiative was that schools could only contribute a part of the resources needed to help poor children and that improved achievement for these children was more related to family income." Department of Health, Education and Welfare, "The Effectiveness of Compensatory Education: Summary and Review of the Evidence," April 1972.

3. See, for example, Lawrence A. Cremin, *The Transformation of the School.*

4. There has been considerable recent propagation of the thesis that schools have no effect on achievement. Much of this arises from public interpretation of *Equality of Educational Opportunity.* See Hanushek and Kain, "On the Value of *Equality of Educational Opportunity.*"

5. An extreme example of problems caused by a fixation on per pupil expenditures is represented in the court remedies for unequal educational opportunity in Washington, D.C. Judge Skelly Wright decreed in the case of *Hobson* v. *Hansen* that the school district was to insure that the per pupil instructional expenditures within all elementary schools were within 5 percent of the district average. The implication of this is that teachers must be distributed in accordance with years of teaching experience, graduate education, and class size—factors which appear to bear little or no relationship to student performance. Further, since the actual per pupil expenditures will be very sensitive to pupil migration throughout the year, considerable teacher transfer and turmoil may be required to adjust "imbalances" during the school session—a situation which will undoubtedly lower student achievement by itself. During the first year of the decree, school year 1971-72, pupil migration during the school year forced some elementary schools outside the 5 percent expenditure band, and the school board—under threat of suit—voted to shift about 100 teachers to different schools when only six weeks remained in the school term. Lawrence Feinberg, "School Board Clears Shifting of Teachers," *Washington Post*, April 26, 1972.

6. The two landmark cases of the past are *Plessy* v. *Ferguson*, 163 U.S. 537(1896) and *Brown* v. *Board of Education of Topeka*, 347 U.S. 483(1954). There have been numerous other less heralded cases, also. A summary of these to 1967 can be found in Meyer Weinberg, *Race and Place* (Washington, D.C.: Government Printing Office, 1967). The range of recent judicial entries can be found in Robert Pressman, "Pending Desegregation Cases," *Inequality in Education* No. 11, March 1972.

7. For example, see "Text of Judge Doyle's Decision," *Denver Post*, May 22, 1970. Here, Judge Doyle states, "A corrollary finding and conclusion was that the segregated core city schools in question were providing an unequal educational opportunity to minority groups as evidenced by low achievement and morale."

8. In particular, see the interpretation in U.S. Commission on Civil Rights, *Racial Isolation in the Public Schools.*

9. For example, see Harvey A. Averch et al., *How Effective Is Schooling?*

10. President's Commission on School Finance, *Schools, People and Money*, pp. 43-47.

11. For example, see Joseph A. Kershaw and Roland N. McKean, *Teacher Shortages and Salary Schedules* (New York: McGraw-Hill, 1962).

12. An exception to this is Henry M. Levin, *Recruiting Teachers for Large City Schools* (mimeograph, The Brookings Institution, 1968).

13. The term accountability, while relatively new in education, appears to have many different meanings. These differences in meanings are somewhat a function of who is being held accountable. For example, this discussion focuses on teachers where others focus on schools or systems. The similar element in the different uses of the term is, however, the interest in relating actions to outcomes and making judgments on outcomes rather than inputs to education. A more general view of accountability can be found in Leon M. Lessinger, "Accountability in Education," in Sterling M. McMurrin (ed.), *Resources for Urban Schools: Better Use and Balance* (New York: Committee for Economic Development, 1971). For a somewhat pessimistic picture of an "accountability experiment," see Office of Economic Opportunity, "An Experiment in Performance Contracting: Summary of Preliminary Results," OEO Pamphlet 3400-5, February 1972.

14. As an example, see National Assessment of Educational Progress, *1969-1970 Science: National Results and Illustrations of Group Comparisons*, Report No. 1 (Washington, D.C.: Government Printing Office, 1970).

15. The case against any form of compensatory education is usually made from a few large attempts at increasing education by large decreases in class size and, usually, a few other frills. Such programs have a large impact on the average cost of education, but, from the previously developed models, cannot be expected to impact much on achievement. The example usually held up to demonstrate the ineffectiveness of compensatory programs is the More Effective School program in New York City; this program halved average class size or, in other terms, doubled average cost. See David J. Fox, "Expansion of the More Effective School Program" (mimeo, New York: Center for Urban Education, 1967). A more general, and more favorable, review of compensatory programs can be found in the Department of Health, Education and Welfare, "The Effectiveness of Compensatory Education."

16. Katzman, *The Political Economy of Urban Schools*; Jencks, "The Conventional Wisdom"; and Owen, "The Distribution of Educational Resources."

17. For a review of current cases and the legal issues involved, see William L. Taylor, "Metropolitan-Wide Desegregation," *Inequality and Education*, No. 11, (March 1972).

18. The President of the United States, "Busing and Equality of Educational Opportunity," March 20, 1972.

19. The results of the METCO program along with other desegregation

programs are summarized in David J. Armor, "The Effect of Busing," *The Public Interest* (Summer 1972).

20. For a discussion of community control, see Henry M. Levin (ed.) *Community Control of Schools* (Washington, D.C.: The Brookings Institution, 1970).

21. For a broader discussion of Mexican-American problems, see Clark S. Knowlton, "The Special Educational Problems of the Mexican-Americans," in Sterling M. McMurrin (ed.), *The Conditions for Educational Equality* (New York: Committee for Economic Development, 1971).

22. Educational voucher proposals build upon the economists' assumptions that the incentives offered by competition lead to the good utilization of resources. An early exposition of the voucher idea can be found in Milton Friedman, "The Role of Government in Education," *Capitalism and Freedom* (Chicago: University of Chicago Press, 1962). A thorough discussion of alternative voucher schemes is given in Center for the Study of Public Policy, *Education Vouchers: A Report on Financing Elementary Education by Grants to Parents* (Cambridge: Center for the Study of Public Policy, 1970).

23. Office of Economic Opportunity, "An Experiment in Performance Contracting."

24. "Black Convention Votes Opposition to Busing Students," *Washington Post*, March 13, 1972; "Nixon on Busing: 'Those Courts Have Gone Too Far'," *Washington Post*, March 17, 1972; and "Meeting of Black Educators Warned on School Apartheid," *Washington Post*, April 1, 1972.

25. A discussion of the rationale for experimentation and a history of some past experiments can be found in Alice M. Rivlin, *Systematic Thinking for Social Action* (Washington, D.C.: The Brookings Institution, 1971), and in John Gilbert and Frederick Mosteller, "The Urgent Need for Experimentation," in *On Equality of Educational Opportunity*. The exact expenditures on experiments or, more broadly, research and development are difficult to pinpoint. Federal R&D expenditures for education are estimated at slightly over $160 million for 1972, or something less than 3 percent of the federal expenditure on education. This is, of course, minute compared to the $9 billion of R&D expenditures for national defense or the $3 billion for space research and technology. See National Science Foundation, "An Analysis of Federal R&D Funding by Budget Function," 1971. R&D expenditures for education from other sources are even more difficult to estimate, but the National Science Foundation places the R&D budget of state and local governments for all functions, not just education, at $500 million in 1971.

26. For a strong statement of this hypothesis see Herbert Gintis, "Education, Technology and the Characteristics of Worker Productivity."

27. A review of past work on the economic role of education can be found in Zvi Griliches, "Notes on the Role of Education in Production Functions and Growth Accounting" in W. Lee Hansen (ed.), *Education, Income and Human Capital*.

Bibliography

Bibliography

Alsop, Joseph. "No More Nonsense About Ghetto Education." *The New Republic*, July 22, 1967.

Armor, David J. "The Effect of Busing." *The Public Interest*, Summer 1972.

_____. "School and Family Effects on Black and White Achievement: A Reexamination of the USOE Data." *On Equality of Educational Opportunity*. New York: Random House, 1972.

Averch, Harvey A. et al. *How Effective Is Schooling?*, R-956-PCSF/RC. Santa Monica: The RAND Corp., 1972.

Barr, Richard H., and Irene A. King. "Bond Sales for Public School Purposes, 1969-70." Washington: Government Printing Office, 1971.

"Black Convention Votes Opposition to Busing Students." *Washington Post*, March 13, 1972.

Bloom, Benjamin S. *Stability and Change in Human Characteristics*. New York: John Wiley and Sons, 1964.

Bowles, Samuel. "Toward An Educational Production Function." In W. Lee Hansen, ed. *Education, Income, and Human Capital*. New York: National Bureau of Economic Research, 1970.

_____and Henry Levin. "The Determinants of Scholastic Achievement—An Appraisal of Some Recent Evidence." *Journal of Human Resources*, Winter 1968.

Break, George. *Intergovernmental Fiscal Relations in the United States*. Washington: The Brookings Institution, 1967.

Burkhead, Jesse. *Input and Output in Large City High Schools*. Syracuse: Syracuse University Press, 1967.

Cain, Glen, and Harold Watts. "Problems in Making Policy Inferences from the Coleman Report." *American Sociological Review*, April 1970.

Carithers, Martha: "School Desegregation and Racial Cleavage, 1954-1970: A Review of the Literature." *Journal of Social Issues* 26, 4.

Center for the Study of Public Policy. *Education Vouchers: A Report on Financing Elementary Education by Grants to Parents*. Cambridge: Center for the Study of Public Policy, 1970.

Cohen, David K.; Thomas F. Pettigrew; and Robert T. Reilly. "Race and the Outcomes of Schooling." In Frederick Mosteller and Daniel P. Moynihan, eds. *On Equality of Educational Opportunity*. New York: Random House, 1972.

Coleman, James S. "Equal Schools or Equal Students." *The Public Interest*, Fall 1966.

Coleman, James S. et al. *Equality of Educational Opportunity*. Washington: Government Printing Office, 1966.

_____ and Nancy L. Karweit. *Measures of School Performance*, R-488-RC. Santa Monica: The RAND Corp., 1970.

Colfax, J. David, and Irving Allen. "Pre-Coded versus Open-Ended Items and Children's Reports of Father's Occupation." *Sociology of Education*, Winter 1967.

Coons, John E.; William H. Clune III; and Stephen D. Sugarman. *Private Wealth and Public Education*. Cambridge: The Belknap Press of Harvard University Press, 1970.

Cravioto, J., and E.R. De Licardie. "The Long-Term Consequences of Protein-Calorie Malnutrition." *Nutrition Reviews*, May 1971.

Cremin, Lawrence A. *The Transformation of the School*. New York: Knopf, 1961.

Cressman, George R., and Harold W. Benda. *Public Education in America*, 3rd Edition. New York: Appleton-Century-Croft, 1966.

Davis, James A. *Undergraduate Career Decisions*. Chicago: Aldine Publishing Co., 1965.

Denison, Edward F. "Measuring the Contribution of Education (and the Residual) to Economic Growth." *The Residual Factor and Economic Growth*. Paris: OECD, 1964.

Farrar, Donald, and Robert Glauber. "The Problem of Multicollinearity Revisited." *The Review of Economics and Statistics*, February 1967.

Feinberg, Lawrence. "School Board Clears Shifting of Teachers." *Washington Post*, April 26, 1972.

Fisher, Franklin M. "On the Cost of Approximate Specification in Simultaneous Equation Estimation." *Econometrica*, April 1961.

_____. "Tests of Equality Between Sets of Coefficients in Two Linear Regressions: An Expository Note." *Econometrica*, March 1970.

Fleischmann, Manley et al. *Report of the New York State Commission on the Quality, Cost and Financing of Elementary and Secondary Education*, 1972.

Fox, David J. *Expansion of the More Effective School Program*. New York: Center for Urban Education, 1967.

Friedman, Milton. *Capitalism and Freedom*. Chicago: University of Chicago Press, 1962.

Gilbert, John P., and Frederick Mosteller. "The Urgent Need for Experimentation." *On Equality of Educational Opportunity*. New York: Random House, 1972.

Gintis, Herbert. "Education, Technology, and the Characteristics of Worker Productivity." *American Economic Review*, May 1971.

Grant, W. Vance, and Kenneth A. Simon. *Digest of Educational Statistics*. Washington: Government Printing Office, 1967.

Griliches, Zvi. "Notes on the Role of Education in Production Functions and Growth Accounting." In W. Lee Hansen, ed. *Education, Income, and Human Capital*. New York: National Bureau of Economic Research, 1970.

_____ and William Mason. "Education, Income, and Ability." Discussion Paper 207, Harvard Institute of Economic Research, 1971.

Guthrie, James et al. *Schools and Inequality*. Cambridge: MIT Press, 1971.

Haller, Emil J. "Pupil Influence on Teacher Socialization: A Socio-Linguistic Study." *Sociology of Education*, Fall 1967.

Hansen, W. Lee; Burton A. Weisbrod; and William J. Scanlon. "Schooling and Earnings of Low Achievers." *American Economic Review*, June 1970.

Hanushek, Eric A. "Efficient Estimators for Regressing Regression Coefficients." (mimeo, 1971).

———. "Regional Differences in the Structure of Earnings." Discussion Paper No. 66, Program on Regional and Urban Economics, Harvard University, 1971.

———. *The Value of Teachers in Teaching*. RM-6362-CC/RC. Santa Monica: The RAND Corp., 1970.

——— and John F. Kain. "On the Value of *Equality of Educational Opportunity* as a Guide to Public Policy." In Frederick Mosteller and Daniel P. Moynihan, ed. *On Equality of Educational Opportunity*, New York: Random House, 1972.

Henderson, James H., and Richard E. Quandt. *Microeconomic Theory*. 2nd Edition. New York: McGraw-Hill Book Co., 1971.

Hilgard, Ernest B. *Theories of Learning*. 2nd Edition. New York: Appleton-Century-Croft, Inc., 1965.

Hunt, J. McV. *Intelligence and Experience*. New York: The Ronald Press Co., 1961.

Illich, Ivan. *Deschooling Society*. New York: Harper and Row, 1971.

Jencks, Christopher S. "The Coleman Report and the Conventional Wisdom." *On Equality of Educational Opportunity*. New York: Random House, 1972.

———. "The Quality of the Data Collected by *The Equality of Educational Opportunity* Survey." *On Equality of Educational Opportunity*. New York: Random House, 1972.

Jensen, Arthur R. "How Much Can We Boost IQ and Scholastic Achievement." *Harvard Educational Review*, Winter 1968.

Johnston, J. *Econometric Methods*. New York: McGraw-Hill Book Co., 1963.

Kain, John F. "The Distribution and Movement of Jobs and Industry." In James Q. Wilson, ed. *The Metropolitan Enigma*. Cambridge: Harvard University Press, 1968.

——— and Joseph Persky. "The North's Stake in Southern Rural Poverty." In John F. Kain and John R. Meyer, eds. *Essays in Regional Economics*. Cambridge: Harvard University Press, 1971.

Katz, Irwin. "Review of Evidence Relating to Effects of Desegregation on the Performance of Negroes." *American Psychologist*, 1964.

Katzman, Martin. *The Political Economy of Urban Schools*. Cambridge: Harvard University Press, 1971.

Kerner, Otto et al. *Report of the National Advisory Commission on Civil Disorders*. Washington: Government Printing Office, 1968.

Kershaw, Joseph A., and Roland N. McKean. *Teacher Shortages and Salary Schedules*. New York: McGraw-Hill, 1962.

Kiesling, Herbert J. "Measuring a Local Government Service: A Study of School Districts in New York State." *The Review of Economics and Statistics*, August 1967.

Knowlton, Clark S. "The Special Educational Problems of the Mexican-Americans." In Sterling M. McMurrin, ed. *The Conditions of Educational Equality*. New York: Committee for Economic Development, 1971.

Kozol, Jonathan. *Death at an Early Age*. Boston: Houghton Mifflin, 1968.

Leary, Mary Ellen. "Are Children Who are Tested in an Alien Language Mentally Retarded?" *The New Republic*, May 30, 1970.

Lessinger, Leon M. "Accountability in Education." In Sterling M. McMurrin, ed. *Resources for Urban Schools: Better Use and Balance*. New York: Committee for Economic Development, 1971.

Levin, Henry (ed.). *Community Control of Schools*. Washington: The Brookings Institution, 1970.

Levin, Henry. "A New Model of School Effectiveness." In U.S. Office of Education, *Do Teachers Make a Difference?* Washington: Government Printing Office, 1969.

———. "Recruiting Teachers for Large City Schools." (mimeo) The Brookings Institution, 1968.

Levy, Frank S. *Northern Schools and Civil Rights*. Chicago: Markham Publishing Co., 1971.

Lurie, Melvin, and Elton Rayack. "Racial Differences in Migration and Job Search: A Case Study." *The Southern Economic Journal*, July 1966.

Maxwell, James A. *Financing State and Local Governments*. Washington: The Brookings Institution, 1965.

McCone, John et al. *A Report of the Governor's Commission on the LA Riots: Violence in the City—An End or a Beginning*, December 1965.

"Meeting of Black Educators Warned on School Apartheid." *Washington Post*, April 1, 1972.

Metz, A. Stafford. "Pupil Mobility in Public Elementary and Secondary Schools during the 1968-69 School Year." Washington: Government Printing Office, 1971.

Moynihan, Daniel P. *The Negro Family: The Case for National Action*. Office of Policy Planning and Research, Department of Labor, 1965.

Mueller, Eva, and William Ladd. "Negro-White Differences in Geographic Mobility." In Louis A. Ferman; Joyce L. Kornbluh; and J.A. Miller, eds. *Negroes and Jobs*. Ann Arbor: University of Michigan Press, 1968.

Mundel, David S. "Modeling the Classroom." (mimeo, 1969).

National Assessment of Educational Progress. *1969-1970 Science: National Results and Illustrations of Group Comparisons*, Report No. 1 Washington: Government Printing Office, 1970.

National Science Foundation. "An Analysis of Federal R&D Funding by Budget Function," 1971.

Netzer, Dick. *The Economics of the Property Tax*. Washington: The Brookings Institution, 1967.

"Nixon on Busing: 'Those Courts Have Gone Too Far'." *Washington Post*, March 17, 1972.

Owen, John. "The Distribution of Educational Resources in Large American Cities." *Journal of Human Resources*, Winter 1972.

Parsons, Talcott. "The School Class as a Social System." *Harvard Educational Review*, Fall 1959.

Pettigrew, Thomas F. *A Profile of the Negro American*. Princeton: D. Van Nostrand, Inc., 1964.

President of the United States. "Busing and Equality of Educational Opportunity." March 20, 1972.

President's Commission on School Finance. *Schools, People, and Money*. Washington: Government Printing Office, 1972.

Pressman, Robert. "Pending Desegregation Cases." *Inequality in Education*, March 1972.

Raab, Earl, ed. *American Race Relations Today*. Garden City, N.Y.: Anchor Books, 1962.

Ravitz, Mel. "The Role of the School in the Urban Setting." In A. Harry Passow, ed. *Education in Depressed Areas*. New York: Teachers College Press of Teachers College, Columbia University, 1963.

Rivlin, Alice. *Systematic Thinking for Social Action*. Washington: The Brookings Institution, 1971.

Sexton, Patricia C. "City Schools." *The Annals of the American Academy of Political and Social Science*, March 1962.

———. *Education and Income*. New York: The Viking Press, 1961.

Shepard, Harold L., and Herbert D. Striner. "Family Structure and Employment Problems." In Louis A. Ferman; Joyce L. Kornbluh; and J.A. Miller, ed. *Negroes and Jobs*. Ann Arbor: University of Michigan Press, 1968.

Silberman, Charles E. *Crisis in the Classroom*. New York: Random House, 1970.

Smith, Marshall. "*Equality of Educational Opportunity:* The Basic Findings Reconsidered." *On Equality of Educational Opportunity*. New York: Random House, 1972.

Stodolsky, Susan B., and Gerald Lesser. "Learning Patterns in the Disadvantaged." *Harvard Educational Review*, Fall 1967.

Taeuber, Karl E., and Alma F. Taeuber. *Negroes in Cities*. Chicago: Aldine Publishing Co., 1965.

Taylor, William L. "Metropolitan-Wide Desegregation." *Inequality in Education*, March 1972.

"Text of Judge Doyle's Decision." *Denver Post*, May 22, 1970.

U.S. Bureau of the Census. *Statistical Abstract of the United States*, 1971. Washington: Government Printing Office, 1971.

U.S. Bureau of the Census. *U.S. Census of Housing, 1960. Volume I, States and Small Areas; Part I, United States Summary*. Washington: Government Printing Office, 1963.

U.S. Bureau of the Census. *U.S. Census of Population 1960. General Social and Economic Characteristics, United States Summary*. Final Report PC(1) - 1C. Washington: Government Printing Office, 1962.

U.S. Bureau of the Census. *U.S. Census of the Population, 1960, Nonwhite Population By Race*. PC(2)-1C. Washington: Government Printing Office, 1963.

U.S. Commission on Civil Rights. *Racial Isolation in the Public Schools*. Washington: Government Printing Office, 1967.

U.S. Department of Health, Education, and Welfare. "The Effectiveness of Compensatory Education: Summary and Review of the Evidence." April 1972.

U.S. Office of Economic Opportunity. "An Experiment in Performance Contracting: Summary of Preliminary Results." OEO Pamphlet 3400-5, February 1972.

U.S. Senate, Select Committee on Equal Educational Opportunity. *Hearings on Equal Educational Opportunity*, 1970.

Weinberg, Meyer. *Race and Place*. Washington: Government Printing Office, 1967.

Weisbrod, Burton A. "Preventing High School Dropouts." In Robert Dorfman, ed. *Measuring Benefits of Government Investment*. Washington: The Brookings Institution, 1965.

_____ and Peter Karpoff. "Monetary Returns to College Education, Student Ability, and School Quality." *The Review of Economics and Statistics*, November 1968.

Weiss, Randall D. "The Effects on Education on the Earnings of Blacks and Whites." *The Review of Economics and Statistics*, February 1970.

Westinghouse Learning Corporation. "The Impact of Head Start." Report to the Office of Economic Opportunity, June 1969.

Wilson, Alan B. "Educational Consequences of Segregation in a California Community." *Racial Isolation in the Public Schools, Appendices*. Washington: Government Printing Office, 1967.

Index

About the Author

Eric Hanushek received his B.S. degree from the U.S. Air Force Academy and his Ph.D. in economics from the Massachusetts Institute of Technology. He has been an Associate Professor of Economics at the U.S. Air Force Academy and has served as a Senior Staff Economist for the Council of Economic Advisers.

His research interests lie in the fields of the economics of education and human resources, urban and regional economics, and econometric methods.